Travel Tips You Can Trust

Anne McAlpin

AAA PUBLISHING

President & CEO	**Robert Darbelnet**
Executive Vice President, Publishing & Administration	**Rick Rinner**
Managing Director, Travel Information	**Bob Hopkins**

Director, Product Development	**Bill Wood**
Director, Sales & Marketing	**John Coerper**
Director, Purchasing & Corporate Services	**Becky Barrett**
Director, Business Development	**Gary Sisco**
Director, Tourism Information Development	**Michael Petrone**
Director, Travel Information	**Jeff Zimmerman**
Director, Publishing Operations	**Susan Sears**
Director, GIS/Cartography	**Jan Coyne**
Director, Publishing/GIS Systems & Development	**Ramin Kalhor**

Product Manager	**Nancy Jones, CTC**
Managing Editor, Product Development	**Margaret Cavanaugh**
Marketing Manager	**Bart Peluso**
AAA Travel Store & E-Store Manager	**Sharon Edwards**
Print Buyer	**Laura Cox**
Manager, Product Support	**Linda Indolfi**
Manager, Electronic Media Design	**Mike McCrary**
Manager, Pre-Press & Quality Services	**Tim Johnson**

Project Coordinator	**Sandy Tate**
Art Director	**Barbra Natali**
Illustrator	**Courtney Canova**
Cover Design	**Joanne McNamara**
Graphic Designer	**Steve Hiller**

Contributing Writer **Christopher Livesay**

Cover Photo	**Dale Durfee/Stone**
Anne McAlpin's Photo on Back Cover	**Christopher Briscoe**

ISBN 1-56251-582-9 Stock Number 144902
Published by AAA Publishing
1000 AAA Drive, Heathrow, Florida 32746

Printed in the USA by RR Donnelley & Sons Company

ABOUT THE AUTHOR

Anne McAlpin is a world traveler, packing expert and author of the popular book and video series *Pack It Up*. Anne has appeared as a featured guest on *Oprah*® and *The View* and continues to make personal appearances across the country. Anne's travel schedule allows her the opportunity to constantly learn new tips and keep informed of the changing security requirements.

Other Books and Videos by Anne McAlpin

Pack It Up

Pack It Up Video

Packing for Adventure Travel Video

Available at www.packitup.com

Other Books by AAA Publishing

Traveling with Your Grandkids

Traveling with Your Pet

AAA Auto Guide: Making Sense of Car Care

AAA Auto Guide: Buying or Leasing a Car

National Park Photography

The Ultimate Fan's Guide to Pro Sports Travel

TABLE OF CONTENTS

PART I: PRE-DEPARTURE — DREAMS AND LOGISTICS

PART III: DESTINATION CONSIDERATIONS

PART IV: COMING HOME

INTRODUCTION
Good travelers are made, not born

Learning how to be one takes time and experience, and it's a life-long process. Whether you're embarking on your first trip or already a seasoned globetrotter, there's always more to know, always a breathtaking wonder of the world you've never seen waiting just over the horizon.

If you can only get yourself there.

This book is for beginning and experienced travelers: singles, doubles and various family combinations of all ages and sizes. That may seem like a diverse group to try and cover in just one book, but I don't think so. Most of us who catch the travel bug when we're young end up becoming many different kinds of travelers in the course of a lifetime. Yesterday's crying baby on the plane is today's embarrassed teenager on the family vacation who is very likely to become tomorrow's parent-with-child in transit.

And any traveler who's come through all of those experiences with the love of travel intact has a great shot at becoming one of those cool senior citizen travelers who's been all over the world and has a million interesting stories to tell.

This book is for you — all of you.

No matter what the demographic, travelers from all walks of life and levels of experience need to use common sense. I have learned a few things about the nature of it in the course of my travels. For starters:

1. Common sense is an acquired skill (like traveling).
2. It doesn't matter if it's acquired secondhand (and it usually is).
3. It doesn't take up any extra space in your bag.
4. It can save you a world of headaches.

I want to share a few tips and opinions with you and show you some good ways to maximize travel's upside by minimizing its potential downside. Travel books are supposed to encourage travel, but there's no way to tell you how to avoid the pitfalls without discussing them honestly: the canceled flight, the lost reservation, the regrettable decision to order the special sauce, and other forms of unexpected "turbulence."

There are plenty of ways to keep such things from happening in the first place or at least to deal with them effectively when they catch you by surprise.

When we travel, we voyage into the unknown — the interesting, the exciting and the unpredictable. It's all part of the journey. And that's usually a good thing. But when it's not, try to remember this: Travel situations that aren't the best experiences can be very helpful lessons learned after the fact. And they often make for the best stories.

Of course, this type of optimism is cold comfort when you're precariously seated in the restroom of a train traveling 60 mph over a rough section of track in southern France and you suddenly discover there's no toilet paper. But we can learn valuable lessons from awkward experiences. Such as . . .

Tip: Always carry one of those travel-size packages of tissues with you. Especially when you travel by train.

Stepping back from specifics for a moment, the guiding principle of traveling well is this: When it comes to encountering the unknown or the unexpected, the prepared traveler is much more likely to experience the joy of serendipity. Being a prepared traveler is more than just knowing what to pack and how to pack it up (although we'll talk about that later). It's knowing how to approach the many facets of travel with common sense, good humor and an independent spirit of adventure, regardless of your age, gender or family dynamics.

Being well-prepared for your trip may not guarantee a smooth ride, but it's the best way I know to steer clear of the bumps in the road.

Happy travels,

Anne

Anne McAlpin
On the road, spring 2002

CHAPTER 1

WHERE DO YOU WANT TO GO?

*Dreaming, planning
and making it happen*

YOU ARE HERE

A word about the book, a few well-traveled opinions for the road and why being a traveler of good common sense matters

Some travel tips were meant to be one-sentence items on a checklist. Others are stories that have to be told. In that sense, this book actually is two books: a practical travel guide, as well as an ongoing personal opinion about how to travel well, no matter how much or how little of it you've done. As a lifelong traveler, I'm committed to making travel a better experience for my fellow travelers.

I have to be honest with you: Of course I want my books to be helpful. But as someone who travels for a living, you travelers out there are the company I keep on any given day. Naturally, I want you all to be well-prepared and happy, not ill-prepared and cranky. By the time you've finished this book, my goal is for you to be traveling lighter, smarter, saving more money and having a much better time in the process.

Almost every great travel tip begins life as some traveler's embarrassing moment. Trial and error is just part of the process of acquiring useful skills, though it can be humbling at times. My philosophy is this: We all pay for our mistakes, so we might as well get something positive out of the transaction.

The good news is, we can. We travelers can learn plenty from our mistakes. The even better news is, we can learn from other people's mistakes so that we don't have to make them ourselves. I believe in learning from mistakes. I also believe in not making them in the first place, and I recommend this strategy to all travelers. It saves time and money, and it's easier on your nervous system. Avoiding potential sources of stress is one of the great secrets of traveling happily. But it's only part of the big picture.

I believe that anyone who is compelled to travel, for any reason, has a lot to gain from becoming what I call *a traveler of good common sense*. Being a traveler of good common sense means different things in different situations. It can mean thoughtful budgeting before you go on your vacation or knowing how to pack for a two-week trip using only carry on-size bags. Sometimes it means keeping your cool in a difficult situation. And sometimes being a traveler of good common sense is as simple or unglamorous as knowing that, in a pinch, a 5-cent resealable plastic bag makes a perfectly fine in-flight toiletry kit.

But we'll get to all of that in a moment. First, we have to decide where we're going.

Common-sense travel traits

Some travel tips are specific to a given situation — use wheeled luggage, apply early for your passport, don't flash large amounts of cash around — while others can be applied to a variety of situations. I have isolated key characteristics of the many common-sense travelers I've met in my years of traveling. Here's the short list:

- Foresight
- Thrift
- Patience

- Humor
- Courtesy
- Flexibility

- Spontaneity
- Vigilance
- Calm

DECIDING WHERE TO GO
Dream big, plan well and start early

It's hard to pinpoint the exact moment when dreaming about a trip becomes planning a trip. There's usually a fair amount of overlap between the two. Good planning is just the practical side of dreaming. If you want to make your travel dreams come true, plan well and start early. There are lots of cost-effective, creative ways to do this, and I recommend a combination of approaches.

PICTURE THIS

Before you start the car or start spending money, start your imagination. Most travel begins as a destination fantasy. What's yours? It could be a white sand beach straight out of a travel magazine photo. Possibly you picture yourself at an outdoor café in Paris sipping red wine, people-watching and catching up on your reading at your own pace.

Perhaps you crave the view of Victoria Falls as seen from a 300-foot bungee-plunge from the zenith of the Victoria Falls Bridge to just above the waterline of the Zambezi River.

Some of us like the experience of being in transit as much as the idea of any particular destination. There's no question that moving scenery can inspire great feelings of personal freedom and possibility, whether it's seen in passing during a pleasure drive across the United States, from the observation car of a train anywhere in the world, from the deck of a cruise ship or through the clouds at 30,000 feet above sea level.

✔ *10 things to do early*

Different tips for different trips. Not all of these may apply to your journey. But once you know where you want to go, here are some things to get a jump on:

☐ Obtain or renew your passport.

☐ Get time off from work.

☐ Book your transportation.

☐ Reserve your accommodations.

☐ Budget! Calculate costs as accurately as you can and make a trip budget.

☐ Start saving for your trip.

☐ Gather information about your destination (books, guides, maps, online research, etc.).

☐ Talk to a travel agent (even if you don't book your trip through one).

☐ Obtain an international driver's permit.

☐ Have a medical and dental checkup. Make sure all prescription medications are up to date and filled. Find out what shots/ immunizations your destination may require.

But wherever our pre-departure flights of imagination take us, the destination is never exactly the way we first pictured it in our mind's eye. Sometimes it's better. Sometimes worse. Always different. So how do you create the best possible odds for realizing your best-case travel scenario? It all starts with two essential ingredients: imagination and good planning. They go well together, and you need to get started early on both of them.

Here are some good ways to do that.

HOW TO PLAN YOUR TRIP

Travel resources online, offline, in person and in print

Here are five key things to do:

1. Start planning and saving early.
2. Find a good travel agent.
3. Read up.
4. Talk to people.
5. Surf the Internet (wisely).

1. Start planning and saving early

Most of us have a long list of places we'd love to see someday. But where should you start? With some basic questions: What do you want to do? How much time do you have? How much money do you have? How much challenge do you want to have on your vacation? Or, how *easy* do you want it to be? Do you want to lie on a beach and watch the waves or vanish for a month in Mexico on a hillside pueblo with just a rucksack of essentials? Do you have a high or low tolerance for risk taking?

Whatever your answer to these questions, the best way to make your trip happen is to begin planning as soon as you can and, whenever possible, to start saving money well in advance. If you're planning to travel internationally, make sure you apply for a passport/visa as soon as you can — preferably at least three months in advance. Once you've applied, passports or visas can easily take six to eight weeks to receive in the mail. You can have the process expedited, but it'll cost you (more on this later).

2. Find a good travel agent

Nothing beats a good travel agent. Some people believe the Internet has replaced the need for them. Not me. I may use the Internet to gather information and comparison shop air fares, but I'm still a believer in working with a travel agent. A good travel agent can save you plenty of time and money. Were they all created equal? Of course not.

But the good ones will listen, ask questions and consistently come up with creative solutions to your particular travel needs without pressuring you to make a decision. So how do you find a good one? Comparison testing, shoppers. Here's an easy method: Call two separate travel agents at random, present them both with the same ticketing request, and see which one of them comes up with the best solution. The one that does, makes the cut.

Depending on the travel agency, it may not cost you anything to

Ask yourself these questions . . .

When you're deciding what you want to do and where you want to go, ask yourself these questions.

• What type of travel do you like? Do you want to drive, fly, take the train or combine methods of transportation?

• What type and level of activity do you enjoy?

• Do you want to travel alone or with someone? Do you want to share a room? If so, smoking or nonsmoking?

• Compatibility. Does the person you're traveling with have similar likes and dislikes?

• Do you want to travel with a tour or group?

• How much do you want to accomplish on your vacation?

• Do you want to relax or see and do as much as possible?

• What type of traveler are you? Do you usually stay in moderately priced hotels or luxury accommodations?

• What would you like to splurge on? What are you willing to economize on?

• Do you prefer elevators where you're staying? Are you willing to walk up a few flights of stairs with your bags?

• What activities do you enjoy on a daily basis? Does your destination offer them?

have an agent check ticket prices and itinerary options for you. And a good travel agent will offer to call you back with the information if you don't have time to hold. Give them the coordinates and see what vector they deliver. But bear in mind that the agent who comes up with the cheapest ticket isn't necessarily the best travel agent.

3. Read up

Reading is a key resource for travelers, and you don't have to spend a fortune to do it. Just find a bookstore with a travel section or, better yet, a good travel bookstore and start browsing. If you have a general idea of where you want to go — Europe, for example — start in that section of the bookstore. Check out the different guidebooks. Look at the maps of the countries and cities that interest you.

Flip through the pages of travel magazines. Spend half an hour in the corner with a cup of coffee and a big picture book of Paris or Nepal.

Pick up a copy of the Sunday paper and read the travel section. Bookstores are great for firing up the traveler's imagination. They can help you with the process of elimination when you're not sure where you want to go. And they can help you find the right guidebook, map or phrase book for your trip once you've chosen your destination.

My No. 1 tip for making a trip happen is this: Buy a book on the destination. For some reason, once I buy a book, I feel like I have to go. It can be very motivational. If you think you might want to go somewhere in particular (such as Barcelona) or only have a general destination in mind (say, Spain), buy a book and leave it out in plain sight. It sits on your table, you keep looking at the beautiful cover, and it gets you thinking, "Gotta go, gotta go, gotta go."

So go. Go through the book with a highlighter or Post-it® notes, write on the pages, read what interests you and skip what doesn't. Then start planning where you'll go, how long you'll stay and whom you want to travel with (or not, solo travelers). A book can get you motivated. It's a reality. You read it, look at the pictures, keep it around the house or leave it on the nightstand and read a chapter every night before you go to sleep. Once you begin to get excited about a destination; you can start making your trip a reality.

If you're tempted to buy out the bookstore and you're worried about blowing your travel budget, go to the public library first. Public libraries are great for helping travelers sort through travel books before they buy.

4. Talk to people

I'm a people person. I enjoy talking to people. I like getting someone's honest opinion about Chicago or Istanbul or Sydney. If you're trying to figure out where to go, ask people who travel: friends, family members, your co-workers. Where did they have a great time? Some friends of mine just got back from Maine. They were very excited about the lobster and the wild beauty of Acadia. It made me want to go there.

People love talking about their travels, and firsthand information can be very helpful. Ask your friends questions. What's their favorite bed-and-breakfast and why? People who know us often know what we like and what we're interested in. When in doubt, ask them to clarify. When you're listening to people's input, be sure you understand what they're saying. Do they like staying in a Motel 6 or at the Four Seasons? Firsthand information also can be a great resource when you're in transit.

5. Surf the Internet (wisely)

Love it or hate it, most of us use the Internet to one degree or another in the course of our lives. When it's good, it's very good. When it's bad, it can misinform or waste valuable time. But the Internet is an incredible resource for travelers.

Whether you're surfing from your personal computer at home so you can print a passport application or logging on in Rome at the combination laundromat/cybercafé to check your e-mail while your socks dry, the Internet has plenty to offer.

My advice to the cyberphobic traveler is this: Relax. Don't be intimidated if you don't have much experience using the Internet. It's not that hard to get the hang of it. You don't have to buy anything or enter your credit card number to find lots of good travel sites and begin pointing and clicking your way through the topics that interest you.

There are entire travel books dedicated to the subject of the Internet. This isn't one of them, so feel free to keep reading. But throughout this book, I'll steer you to sites that I think are particularly helpful when they're relevant to the topics being discussed in a chapter.

One of the Internet's great blessings to the traveler is the ability it gives you to instantly check information, such as the latest State Department reports and travel advisories for any country in the world. If you tried to put all of that information into book form, it would be an encyclopedia — half of it outdated by the time you got it into print. But with the Internet, you can get an instant update on any country in the world, or you can just check today's high temperature in Rio.

There are, however, some things to keep in mind about the Internet. Current information is essential to the traveler, and there's no shortage of it online. But what do you really need to know? What can you afford to ignore? And what's true? The Internet can be very useful, informative and fun for trip planning and do-it-yourself bookings.

For many, it's an essential resource for last-minute travel arrangements. But check your facts. Don't assume anything is gospel truth just because you see it in print online. Many of your favorite "brick-and-mortar" travel book publishers and travel organizations, including AAA, have very helpful sites. If there's a name you trust in the *offline* world, try searching for that business or organization's website first before clicking on a banner ad promoting *fly-by-night-really-super-cheap-fares.com*.

Before you go, plan your trip well in advance

1. Do your homework when you think of a destination. Find out as much as you can about the area, places of interest and local customs. Study the brochures of the travel company you're interested in and write down any questions you might have so you don't forget to ask.
2. Form a lasting relationship with a travel agent.
3. Make your plans six to eight months in advance to get the best prices and availability.
4. Pay attention to the small details now — seat assignments, special meal requests, frequent flyer numbers, seating for cruises and other details.
5. Be aware of the entry requirements for the country you're visiting. Passports should be valid for six months past your return date to the States. Find out now about visa requirements. Your travel agent should provide this information and assistance in having visa's processed.
6. Check with your physician or local health department and ask about health precautions or vaccinations that may be required or suggested for your trip.

Susan Ledford
AAA General Manager
Hendersonville Service Office, N.C.

Whatever you decide, start planning as soon as you can. And, once again, if your plans include overseas or international travel, be sure you've got a current passport before you buy that $400 bargain fare to London. Departure day? This Friday.

Oops. Nonrefundable ticket.

Dream big, but be realistic about the kind of traveler you are.

If you haven't traveled extensively, don't stress yourself out at the starting gate. Don't jump into something that's really difficult. If you've never left the country, it's probably not a great idea to begin with a culture that's completely alien to you or go somewhere where you don't speak the language and nobody speaks your language.

If you're not an experienced traveler, try a weekend of car camping or a trip to the shore before canoeing your way into the Amazon rainforest. It's easier to pack a car than a suitcase, which has space limitations. If you have a real problem with packing, start with a weekend away before you jump right into a five-day walking trek of the Inca Trail and Machu Picchu high in the Peruvian Andes.

PLANNING FAMILY TRIPS

This is a big topic. So big, it gets its own chapter. (See Chapter 9, Tips and Tactics for Sane Family Travel.) There are certain great democratic principles that can be applied to all kinds of group travel, whether you're traveling with a college friend, spouse, children, grandchildren or grandparents. We'll talk about those principles as well as ways families can travel together without going broke or driving each other crazy in the process.

Pacing your trip, pacing your day

Pace your vacation days wisely. If you're traveling with children or seniors, consider how much stamina they have. For that matter, consider how much stamina *you* have. It's better to plan a few key activities that everyone will enjoy than to exhaust the whole group by trying to do too much.

That goes for in-transit days, too. If you spend 14 hours flying to New Zealand through seven time zones, don't expect to take in a long sightseeing tour right off the plane. You might need a nap first. Then again, a walk might be just the thing to shake off the jet lag (before you sleep for 12 hours straight without moving once). Whatever your pace, whatever your preference, know before you go and plan your days accordingly.

If you pace yourself, are realistic about what you can do and remain flexible, you'll be a lot happier. Most travelers find that they build up stamina as a trip goes along. You get excited, and you get into the swing of things. But it can take a few days to shake off home, work and jet lag, to get used to a new territory, new people, different food. Everything in your system needs time to adjust. Let it. Don't worry, you'll still have plenty of time to enjoy your vacation. And so what if you don't get to every last thing on your itinerary? Your trip won't be a failure because you spend the afternoon walking through the farmer's market eating fresh olives and feta cheese instead of parasailing on the beach.

The key is not to stress yourself unnecessarily with unreasonable expectations about what you can or *must* do. A friend might say, "You're going to _____? (fill in your destination of choice here).

Consider these opinions about the Internet

 Try to keep in mind at least some of the following as you point and click your way across the globe.

Here are five opinions about the Internet for the traveler to consider:

1. **It shouldn't be your only resource for travel planning.** Variety is not only the spice of life, it's a smart way to approach travel information resources. Don't just be a "mouse potato" surfing the Internet. Talk to people, read, watch travel documentaries and use your imagination.

2. **It's not *always* faster or cheaper.** For example: These days, if you have a dial-up connection instead of a high-speed direct connection, the Internet isn't necessarily faster than being your own personal browser in a good travel bookstore or just talking with someone. (And high-speed, direct connections to the Internet aren't free — or even cheap, depending on your household budget.)

3. **Many websites are trying to sell you something.** It's true of course, but ...

4. **That's not necessarily a bad thing.** Hey, I've found some very handy travel gizmos while surfing travel sites. You can find a lot of very useful information from sites geared toward turning a profit. But, as with all modes of shopping anywhere, the golden rule is always *let the buyer beware.* Just use your good judgment. The vast majority of consumers still prefer to use the Internet for research rather than for making purchases.

5. **You don't have to own a computer to make good use of one.** Many public libraries offer free or inexpensive online access, and cybercafes can be a convenient, affordable alternative to buying a computer or schlepping one around the world.

Don't bite off more than you can chew

Rome wasn't built in a day, so don't try to see it in one.

Pacing is one of the most important things to consider when you're planning your trip. We all want to get the most out of our travel experience and our budget, but running yourself ragged isn't the way to do it.

I remember a conversation I had with a weary traveler back in the days when I worked as a tour director. This poor woman was on an incredibly ambitious, 25-day bus tour of Europe — and that's a long time to spend on a bus *anywhere*.

"It's wonderful how much I've seen," she said, sounding more tired than wonderful, "but it's absolutely *exhausting*." And she did indeed look exhausted.

"You can take a day off," I said. "You can stay in the hotel and have a cup of tea and read your book."

"I *can?*" she said, looking sort of amazed and relieved and slightly guilty all at the same time.

"Of course you can. It's your vacation. Do what you want. Give yourself a break."

She seemed very pleased. "Well . . . *thank you.*"

I felt like I'd given her permission to do what she really wanted to do.

A few years later, I had to remember my own advice. I was on a 21-day trek of Nepal, part of which went through a jungle. It was a beautiful trip, but exhausting at times. One afternoon, there was a bird-watching tour through the jungle. I thought, "I'd really rather stay at the lodge and enjoy a book from their incredible library." So I did.

It was a very long trip. I already was having a very full experience. That's why so many people end up saying, "I need a vacation from my vacation." Even on a luxury cruise ship, people end up saying that. It's not necessary. When you're on vacation, it's OK to be on vacation.

We went there last year! You *have* to go to this great little place..." And we feel like we really do have to go there.

But we don't.

This is the flip side of asking people about their travel experiences. You can learn a lot from firsthand stories, but you don't have to do what they did. I think good planning means being well-prepared for any number of possibilities, including the ones you couldn't have...well...*planned*. In other words, spontaneity is the spice of travel life, so leave a little room for it in your bag. If you don't like it, you'll still have your list.

Decide where you'd like to go. And when you know the answer, *your* answer, turn the page, and we'll start considering transportation options.

CHAPTER 2

How Do You Want to Get There?

*Modes of transportation,
points of departure*

What type of transportation should you use?

Now that you've figured out where you want to go, how should you get there? Like so many other travel recipes, transportation boils down to two key ingredients: time and money. How much of them do you have? How (and where) do you want to spend them?

If you have more time than money, a bus, coach, train or cruise ship all can be good options. If the reverse is true, flying usually is the method of choice. And if you're going on summer vacation with two kids, a dog, 10 suitcases and an elaborate connect-the-dots itinerary of friends and relatives in six different states, well...just make sure you've changed the oil in the car recently. And read Chapter 9, Tips and Tactics for Sane Family Travel, before you go.

Have you considered all the options?

First, let's sort out a few common biases and misunderstandings that plague certain forms of transportation. If you're one of those people who cringes at the thought of bus travel, you should be aware of what coach tours have to offer. There's a big difference between a bus trip and a coach tour, and it helps to know what that difference is.

I've also talked to many younger travelers who have never been on a cruise ship because of their preconceived notions. They don't realize that cruise ship travel can be a blast for all ages.

As for train travel...people who've never ridden trains sometimes imagine them to be just like the bus. They aren't. For one thing, they've got a lot more bathrooms. A note about my mentioning bathrooms in this book: Knowing where to find them and dealing with them when you find them in a less-than-ideal condition is just a fact of life for all travelers.

You can get up, move around, go to the observation car for a beer and a sandwich, some scenery, reading or conversation. Or have dinner in the dining car. You can ride coach if you're on a budget or get your own sleeping compartment if you want to splurge on a bit of luxury.

Obviously, some destinations eliminate certain options. Want to go to Australia? You know you won't be driving or taking the train. But when you do have a choice, consider which mode of transportation best matches your trip, your time and your patience (not to mention your wallet). And be ready to mix and match modes of transportation accordingly.

SUBMITTED FOR YOUR CONSIDERATION
Planes, trains, cars, cruise ships and coaches
Planes

I realize that some people are apprehensive about flying, but it's still the safest, fastest way to get where you're going. And it's still the best way to maximize the time you can spend at your destination. If you don't care about the scenery between point A and point B, but you just want to be on the beach now, you can't beat flying.

Yes, flying has its drawbacks: Airline food always will be a punchline waiting to happen; there never will be enough leg room in coach; and how much sound quality did you really expect to get out of a $1 pair of plastic headphones? However, there are many ways to beat jet lag, calm your nerves, minimize baggage-related hassles, avoid boredom, maximize your leg room, deal with the food and/or get the best fare. We'll talk about all of those things, as well as what you need to know about airport security regulations (see Chapter 12, Air Travel).

No matter which method of transit floats your boat, a common-sense traveler always should consider the following questions before making a decision:

1. How much time do you have?
2. How much money do you have?
3. Are you on a schedule? And . . .
4. If so, how fixed or flexible is it?
5. Is there a method of travel you've always wanted to try? (Train? Cruise ship?)
6. Is there a method you'd rather avoid? (Flying? Driving?) And, if so . . .
7. Are you able to avoid it? (If the answer is "no," see corresponding chapters for ways to minimize problems associated with your method of transportation.)
8. How much stuff do you need to bring with you?
9. Are you traveling alone or with family?
10. Are you traveling with pets?

Trains

I think every traveler should experience at least one serious train trip in their lifetime. (Commuter trains and subway rides don't count.) Taking the train can be an extremely rich, but not necessarily *expensive*, travel experience if you have time on your hands, want to watch the scenery go by without having to drive and are not too attached to a strict arrival time. Europe and North America still have the best rail systems in the world, with Eurail and Amtrak offering a variety of flexible, money-saving passes and different levels of luxury, privacy and economy, with correspondingly priced fares.

But Eurail and Amtrak certainly aren't the only ways to get around by rail. There are train systems throughout the world, with options as diverse as a luxury rail journey through British Columbia, Canada or the rough-and-tumble cheap seats on the roof of the train in India or Ecuador. I'm also an advocate of using subway systems as a cost-effective, time-saving way to travel in big cities. For more details on train travel and how to go about it, see Chapter 14 , Trains and Rails.

Cars

Individuality, freedom of mobility and the road trip all are big parts of the American dream. Our longstanding love of the automobile and the interstate are manifestations of this dream, even if things get a bit jammed up now and then. Cars can be a less-expensive mode of transportation for family travel than the plane, depending on your destination. But don't forget to add in gas, food and lodging costs when making your budget. Know your miles-per-gallon ratio, get a good road atlas and calculate the distance you have to travel. How long will it take you? Where will you stay along the way? And, most importantly, be safe. Make sure your car is in sound mechanical condition before you hit the road.

Driving is a good way to go if you've got the time, if you have to take a lot of things with you or if your itinerary is so complex it would cost you $27,000 in air fares to make the same trip by plane with a family of four. You can choose your own path, be on your own schedule and show the kids the sights. If you're traveling with pets, car travel can be much less traumatic for them than plane travel, as long as you let them out for regular walks, give them enough water and never leave them in the car unattended. For tips on traveling happily with your pets, see Chapter 9, Tips and Tactics for Sane Family Travel.

As for rental cars...

If you want all of the advantages of having a car available at your destination but don't want to drive there, then rent a car when you arrive. But consider this option carefully. If you're spending a weekend in San Francisco and always dreamed of sightseeing on Highway 1 along the Pacific coast, a rental might be perfect for you. If you've never navigated a rotary in Rome or experienced the vehicular dyslexia of driving on the left side of the road in merry (and for some American drivers, *scary*) old England...well, you may find the train or a motor coach a much better way to get around. For more information about rental cars and road trips, see Chapter 13, Car Travel.

Cruise ships

Cruising is a wonderfully relaxing but fun way to see a wide variety of destinations and scenery with a minimal amount of effort on your part. You don't have to pack and unpack. Generally, everything is included except your extras and alcohol. So it's easier on your budget because you know how much you're going to be spending right up front. Cruise ships also can be an extremely good value for family leisure travel because they offer package deals and facilities that accommodate all age groups. But you do have to know what to look for, what to avoid and how to pick them. And, yes, we'll talk about how to do all that, too. See Chapter 16, Cruising the World.

Coaches and buses

Viva la difference! If you like road trips but you don't want to do the driving yourself, let someone else do it for you. Coach tours can be an excellent way to get around. You don't have to worry; you just sit on the bus and watch the world go by. They're a bargain, they're an essential and helpful source of mass transit all over the globe, and in some parts of the world they're the only option. But there's a big difference between a bus trip and a coach tour. While a bus trip generally is a random assortment of passengers, stops and starts, a coach tour usually is comprised of a group of leisure travelers with a common interest and destination — which makes things a lot more fun. Coach tours are an excellent way to see a lot of interesting sites (especially in cities) with a minimum amount of stress.

Many coach tours feature tour guides who can answer your questions and supply a travelogue to go with the sites. True, they aren't for everyone. Many travelers enjoy the exertion and independence of seeing a city on their own and exploring on foot. Nothing wrong with that. But a coach tour doesn't have to be a crowd scene. There also are mini-coach tours that are geared for only 12 to 15 people. Many people love mini-coach trips because they're not with 40 or 50 other passengers, which some people find overwhelming. For more information, read Chapter 15, Leave the Driving to Them.

Ready to book your trip?

Once you've considered your destination and transportation options, it's time to think about booking your trip. Maybe you want to do that yourself; maybe you want a travel agent to handle all the details; or maybe you want to do some of it yourself and let a travel agent take care of the rest. Whichever method you prefer, we'll get to it.

CHAPTER 3

BOOKING YOUR TRIP

*Ways and means
to an end*

TIMING IS EVERYTHING

There's a joke/truism about the three most important things in real estate being location, location, location. A variation of this principle applies to booking your ticket to ride. The three most important things are: start early, start early, start early. This isn't always possible. And when it's not, try not to fret. But be prepared to pay more. The earlier you can begin making reservations, the more money you'll save and the more room you'll leave yourself to maneuver. Unless you like to take advantage of last-minute travel bargains.

How should you book your trip?

You have three choices:
1. Do it yourself.
2. Have a travel agent do it for you.
3. Combine the first two approaches.

1. Booking it yourself

It helps to know what you're doing before taking this route. If the process is new to you, start small before booking everything for a big trip yourself. Research is the best place to begin.

• Talk to travel agents and have them send you free brochures on any destination that interests you. Ask them to price fares for you.

• Call a few airlines at their toll-free numbers. Comparison shop fare prices and inclusions before making any reservations. Sometimes travel agencies have the best deals because they can offer incentives for bookings.

• Go online. Check out different travel websites including AAA's website. If you're not new to this, check AAA's website anyway. It's a gold mine of travel information.

• Read up on destinations that interest you.

In other words, don't go in cold. Arm yourself with knowledge. Be informed. This chapter includes some of the best tips I know of for booking transportation.

Starting the process early is an especially good strategy if you're new to booking your own reservations. Minimize the pressure on yourself by giving yourself plenty of time to look around and comparison shop. You're less likely to feel like you have to jump on a particular fare if you're not in a rush. Don't be intimidated: None of this is brain surgery. You'll be surprised how fast you get comfortable asking questions, checking fare prices and calling (or surfing) around. Don't let anyone pressure you into making a reservation and/or a ticket purchase if you're not ready to.

2. Booking through a travel agent

A good travel agent is more than someone who can use the computer while they talk on the phone. A good travel agent has been there, done that, got the T-shirt and can tell you what you need to know — both as a professional and as a traveler with firsthand experience. Don't settle for less, because you don't have to. It's a competitive business.

If you're well-traveled and prefer to make your own reservations, do it on the Internet or call the airline directly. If you're not well-traveled, I suggest talking with a good travel agent for starters.

Here's one of the best ways I know to qualify how good a travel agent or agency is: Find out whether your agent has been to the destination they hope to sell you a ticket to. This matters, especially with any sort of exotic travel. If you're going on a photo safari in Africa, for example, make sure your agent (or someone in the agency whom you can talk with) has been there. Don't go to a travel agent who's never been on a cruise if you're booking a cruise. People do this sort of thing all the time, and it makes no sense. Find an agent who specializes in the destination that interests you and pick their brain.

Some people like to let a travel agent handle *all* of their travel arrangements. There are advantages to this. You can give the agent your travel dates, budget parameters, destination and accommodation preferences, and wait for them to call you back with options and a price. Again, comparison shop. Call a couple of agents, give them the same information, see what they come up with and don't purchase your ticket until you have a number of answers to compare from different sources.

Five things good travel agents do

1. Listen to you.
2. Ask questions to get to know your travel needs.
3. Get back to you quickly.
4. Offer you alternatives, but let you decide.
5. Treat you with courtesy no matter what your level of travel experience is.

3. Combining the two approaches

Ultimately, I feel mixing and matching is the best of both worlds for experienced and inexperienced travelers. Yes, work with a travel agent, but take an active role in planning, researching and booking your own trip and accommodations. The more you know, generally speaking, the more money you'll save. Make sure the agent is getting you the best price. Compare the answers you've come up with to your travel agent's advice and then decide which way to go.

The more you travel, the more you learn. And the more you learn, the more comfortable you will become handling your own arrangements. Most importantly, whether you end up booking your own trip or not, you learn how to ask travel agents the right questions, and together you can come up with better answers to your individual travel needs. With the advent of airline commission caps and consumer access to online booking, travel agents know they have to be competitive — which means they have to bring experience and knowledge to the table or lose clients.

How best to mix and match? I use the Internet, I call the airlines, and I look at the latest fares and bargains being advertised in the travel section of the Sunday paper. But even after many years and miles of travel, I still use travel agents and still find them an incredibly important resource.

Translating airline-speak

Direct, nonstop and connecting flights. The differences and why you need to know them.

So you got a "direct flight" for a bargain price? Terrific! That'll save time, right? Well . . . no, actually not. Sorry. "But what could possibly be more direct than a 'direct flight?'" you ask, quite reasonably. Here's the scoop:

Direct: A direct flight means same airline, same plane but one or more stops along the way to your final destination.

Nonstop: Just what it sounds like, a flight with no stops. In other words, nonstop is more direct than a direct flight.

Connecting flight: A flight that stops and requires you to change planes on the way.

Saving money, time and hassle

Some of these tips are mode-of-transportation specific; others are general principles. This is by no means a complete list, and there are exceptions to every rule. But it's a good starting point for the inexperienced and hopefully will have one or two pieces of information that you more experienced travelers didn't know.

Tip 1: You guessed it . . . start early

Q: How early?

A: The sooner the better.

There's no hard and fast rule for how far in advance you should book your trip. But the sooner you can do it, the better. And the cheaper, too. Making reservations four to six months in advance of your trip is ideal if you can muster it. The first rule about fares is this: The closer you make your reservation to your departure day, the higher the fare. The more time you give yourself, the more chance you'll have of getting the best fare *and* the travel dates you want. This is especially true for any peak travel times, like summer and Thanksgiving through New

The right travel agent for you

How do you know if you have the right travel agent? One of the first clues will be what your agent wants to know about you. A savvy agent will want to find out a great deal about you, your traveling companions and why you want to travel in the first place. Expect myriad questions about your likes and dislikes, the comfort level you require in lodgings and transportation, and the amenities you expect while on the road. And be prepared to discuss the objectives of your trip whether it's for relaxation, adventure, education or for other reasons.

The agent also should inquire about how flexible you want to be in order to obtain greater value. On your part, answer your agent's questions as thoroughly as you can. The better the agent knows you, the more successful the agent can tailor your arrangements to your particular needs.

AAA Travel Products & Services
Costa Mesa, Calif.

Year's. Many parents, for example, wisely book holiday passage for their college-attending kids the week classes start.

Tip 2: Look before you book

Everyone's heard the saying "look before you leap." When it comes to transportation, my advice is: Look before you book. Consider your options carefully before you commit to any one method of transportation or another. Don't get stuck in the one-mode-of-transportation-fits-all way of thinking at the expense of your trip. Creative combinations can expand your possibilities and help you get more out of your trip, your time and your travel budget. Travel agents can be invaluable to this process.

Tip 3: Make sure you can get away before you buy your ticket

So, you've got a bunch of paid vacation hours socked away? Great. But can you use them? It's not just the vacation time you've accrued, but whether or not you can get the time off around the dates you've planned. Confirm your vacation dates at work *before* you buy your ticket

Whether you book it or they book it

 Here's something I discovered on my first trip to Europe, and I've always followed this plan ever since: When you're planning your trip, mix up the time you spend in the country and the city. Too much of either environment can be too much of a good thing, in my experience. Try two days in rural locations, two days in the city, for example.

People often don't think about this balance until they're on day five of a tour of European capitals and they're about to go insane from the noise, traffic and crowds. Rome, for example, is a wonderful, beautiful city, but it can be frantic to the point that you're not getting the relaxation you need from a vacation.

Conversely, if you're the type of person who thrives on city life, don't book two weeks in a Swiss chalet miles from the city, or you may find yourself craving more excitement.

Whatever environment you prefer, consider the balance and make sure you get what you need from your trip.

and, preferably, before you make your reservation. This may seem obvious, but it's surprising how many people get caught in this bind. Once you've made your reservation, airlines require you to purchase your (nonrefundable) ticket within 24 hours.

Tip 4: Traveling during the week can save you money

Can you fly Monday through Thursday, instead of flying on a Friday, Saturday or Sunday? If so, do it. It will save you money. Again, tips like this one are a general rule, but that doesn't mean there aren't exceptions. If you *can* fly during the week, ask the airline ticketing agent or your travel agent to compare fares and see where the savings are.

Creative mixing and matching

Make the most of your trip.

I know a couple in Seattle who always had wanted to ride the Alaska Marine Highway ferry through the Inside Passage from Bellingham, Wash., to Sitka, Alaska, in the month of May (when the weather is nice but neither the tourists nor the black flies are out in great numbers yet).

It's a beautiful trip through the Pacific Northwest coastal islands and inlets of Washington State, British Columbia and southeast Alaska. But with stops along the way from Ketchikan to Wrangell to the state capitol in Juneau, it's not a trip for anyone who's in a big hurry.

Unfortunately, this two-career couple could find only a week to spare between them in the month they wanted to travel. Their creative solution was to ride the ferry from its departure point in Bellingham, Wash., to Sitka, Alaska, where they stayed for a few days before taking a one-way flight back to Seattle. Since the ferry didn't depart until late afternoon, they decided to take the inexpensive and beautiful train ride that runs up the eastern shore of Puget Sound from Seattle to Bellingham (where the train stops practically across the street from the Alaska Marine Highway ferry terminal/departure point).

Using this mix-and-match approach, they were able to make the most out of the limited time they had while still enjoying the relaxed pace of train and ferry travel. The moral of the story is: Be creative, be flexible, and you'll get more for your time and your money.

Five good reasons to use a travel agent

1. Free research assistance

This is an area where a travel agent can be extremely helpful in the planning stage of your trip. They know about all sorts of package deals, family plans, rail and coach or cruise ship and coach combinations that can stretch your budget and your itinerary in ways you might not have imagined. I reiterate this money-saving tip: Putting a travel agent on the case to research options doesn't require you to buy anything, but some agents charge a fee for this service. And it doesn't prevent you from researching your own ideas online or in print. It just gives you more options to work with.

2. Airline updates and backup plans

If an airline goes on strike, are you going to call them while you're in Europe on your vacation and try to confirm that you have a way home? A travel agent can take care of problems like this, in advance. You could just call them and say, "Hey, I hear No-Fly Airlines is going on strike. Can you tell me what's up?" Or your agent would contact you in advance of the fact and help you make alternate arrangements.

3. Save time, save money

I continually remind travelers: Your time is money, too. You might be able to get yourself as good a deal on your own, but an experienced travel agent often can get you the same deal or a better one in a third of the time. Travel agents are full-time travel professionals.

4. Scam-proof your trip

Agents offer tips on avoiding scams and can help you find lodgings around the world to help you minimize potential hassles. Avoid shady operators and fly-by-night agencies. Go with an agency you can trust and that has a long history of protecting travelers.

5. Current information

The benefit of a travel agency is that it can provide you updated information about any destination you're interested in. If a war's about to break out or a hurricane is brewing in your favorite tropical utopia, the agency knows all these things or can find out. Travel agents know it's in their best interest to look out for your best interests.

Tip 5: Fly with the night owls

If you don't mind staying up late, "red-eye" flights can save you money. As a rule, airlines base their pricing on the free-market principle of supply and demand: The higher the demand, the higher the price. Late-night flights generally are considered less desirable and, therefore, often are discounted. Obviously, don't expect to arrive fresh as a daisy at 4 a.m. But if you don't mind the wilt factor, "the red-eye" can save you green.

Tip 6: The best day — and time — of the week to get a cheap airfare

Airfare wars tend to peak midweek, offering a brief window of opportunity to grab a cheap ticket before they're all spoken for or the price goes up again. The same savings-through-sleep-deprivation principle as flying the "red-eye" is at work here. If you don't mind staying up late in order to save some money, try making your reservation around 1 a.m. on a Wednesday (meaning, after midnight on a Tuesday night).

Tip 7: Travel off-season and save money

Just as midweek travel is cheaper than weekend travel, off-season travel can save you a bundle. The key time for off-season budget travel is the second week of January through early spring. Summer is the peak travel season, of course. But come late September, the school year begins for millions of people, from kindergartners to college students. Everyone wraps up their summer vacations, and there are travel specials to be had until the Thanksgiving rush begins. Fall and spring can be great times to travel if you can get away. The weather in many places still is great, and there are fewer tourists. Not only can you beat the crowds by traveling off-season, but the locals often are more relaxed and friendlier than they are during the peak tourist season.

Tip 8: It never hurts to ask, and you might get a break

Don't be shy. When making reservations — either directly or through a travel agent — you always should ask: "Can you find a better rate?" The worst that can happen is they'll say "no." But you'd be surprised how many times that simple question can shake loose a better price on transportation fares, hotel rates, rental car rates, etc.

It's not the end of the world if you have to change your reservation after you've purchased your ticket, but it could cost $75-$100 every time you do, depending on the airline. Notice, I say can. Always plead your case if you have to change a reservation. Ticketing agents can give you a break on the change fee, and sometimes they will.

Translating airline-speak

Explaining nonrefundable tickets
A nonrefundable ticket doesn't mean you're out of luck if you don't use it on the scheduled date. It just means you can't get your money back for the price of the ticket. But the ticket price can be applied to a rescheduled flight — usually minus a $75 fee for changing the reservation.

Tip 9: Consider all possible discounts

How many frequent flyer miles have you accrued? Is there a discount for children and/or seniors? Do they offer a discount for AAA members? Is there a group rate? A family package? An off-season discount? This tip is an extension of Tip 8. Work every angle. Never assume a person on the other end of the phone knows your particular situation (i.e., that you're a senior, for example) and don't be afraid to ask questions.

Tip 10: Cheaper is not always better

A lesson we touched on in Chapter 1. Time is money, too. Don't save a hundred bucks by adding loads of extra time and stops to your flight (as many discounted tickets do) unless for some reason you really want to or absolutely can't afford not to. It's hard to calculate the price of stress, but peace of mind is invaluable. To that end, if there's a particular airline you trust or feel more comfortable flying with, then go with them — even if it costs a bit more.

BOOKING ACCOMMODATIONS

Where to stay once you're there

There are a number of principles that apply to making any kind of reservation, whether it's transportation or accommodations. These principles include: don't be afraid to ask, look for the discount and there are others. But reserving accommodations has its own set of tips, rules and helpful guide lines. Accordingly, it gets its own chapter. Read on.

CHAPTER 4

ROOM AND BOARD

*Reservations, accommodations,
meals, deals and assorted handy tips*

LODGING CONSIDERATIONS

Hotels and lodgings are as varied as the world and the people who travel in it. So you need to consider what kind of traveler you are, how much money you can spend and how adventurous you want to be when seeking out accommodations. Do you want a sure bet, a unique experience or a combination of the two? Hotels are kind of like restaurants in this respect. With big chains, there's the comfort and security of knowing what you're getting ahead of time, but it's more predictable, too. A cheeseburger from McDonald's® is pretty much the same whether you get it in Athens, Ga., or Athens, Greece. The same thing is true of rooms at most big hotel chains around the world. Ask yourself: How far off the beaten path do you want to go? How unique an experience do you want from your lodgings?

Should you book in advance or wing it?

Some people wouldn't dream of going on vacation without knowing exactly where they'll be staying when they get there. There are good arguments to be made for this approach. If you're traveling with your family to Walt Disney World® Resort in July, you'd be well-advised to know where you're staying ahead of time. If you're riding the trains in Europe on a Eurailpass and not on a fixed itinerary, you may feel perfectly comfortable playing it by ear and looking for interesting hotels wherever you happen to get off the train. Either way, consider your options — and your comfort level with the unknown — before you go.

Find the balance you're comfortable with

It's up to you to decide the lodging strategy you're most comfortable with — sure bet or improvisation. And like so many things in the world of travel (preferred methods of payment, travel agents vs. booking it yourself, etc.), I'm more of a mix-and-match person than a one-answer-fits-all person. I prefer to have my accommodations squared away for at least the first night I'll be staying at my destination. It's pretty daunting to arrive somewhere new — especially in a foreign country — and not know where you'll be spending the night. However, once you've settled in, exploring the options and seeing what you can find on your own can be a fine adventure, especially in the off-season when accommodations are more readily available.

Finding accommodations and making reservations online: pros and cons

The convenience factor is a big plus, of course. Many hotels (and not just the chains), country inns, spas, and bed-and-breakfasts have their own websites where you can see current rates, find maps and directions, click on pictures of the accommodations, make your reservations online and contact the proprietors via e-mail. But there are thousands of great hotels throughout the world that aren't online. They can't afford to be computerized. They're small-time operations, often family businesses that offer unique accommodations and true local flavor — but no e-mail or websites.

This is where guidebooks come in handy

Guidebooks are a good way to check out hotel accommodations that are offline and off the beaten path, as well as the mainstream ones. A word of caution: Hotel rates often change faster than guidebooks can go to print. Always double-check. And just as there are many terrific accommodations that can't be found online, there are plenty of great hotels you won't see in the guidebooks. That one fact alone often makes them cheaper, but harder to find.

Before you leave for your trip, you may want to make a reservation at a place with a liberal cancellation policy (say, no charge as long as you give 24 hours' cancellation notice), then find a better deal or a more interesting local hotel once you get to your destination and can look around for yourself. This way, you know you're covered if you don't find anything, but you've got the flexibility to be spontaneous if you find a quaint hotel, an interesting inn or a bed-and-breakfast you can't resist.

What's your price range?

This seems like a simple question, but it's one that people often quantify strictly in terms of dollar amount per night equals one standard of lodging for my entire trip. But that approach can be limiting. Here's a suggestion: Start by figuring out the total amount of money you want to budget for your trip accommodations and divide it by the number of nights you need lodging. Have you decided you want to (or have to) live on a budget for your entire trip, or do you want to splurge? Maybe you can do a bit of both.

This doesn't have to be an either/or question. Once again, creative mixing and matching can expand your possibilities. Maybe you want to economize with a budget hotel, a hostel or camping for a couple of nights and then splurge on a night or two at a bed-and-breakfast, a luxury hotel or a spa. If you can plan in advance to spend less than your allotted daily budget for a portion of your trip, you'll be able to go over your daily average and indulge yourself a bit for a night or two. This also can be a workable compromise for traveling companions who have different accommodation priorities.

What amenities do you need?

The North American standard and the rest of the world: Most hotel rooms in North America, even the economy ones, have their own bathroom and (usually) come with air conditioning. If this is the minimum standard of comfort and privacy you require when you travel, be aware that it costs much more to maintain it in other parts of the world. A private bath can add significantly to the cost of your lodgings outside of North America.

Getting the right room

Whether you're making a reservation by phone or just showing up at the front desk looking for a room, these tips can help you have a more pleasant stay:

1. If you have a problem with noise, get an inside courtyard room whenever possible, not an outside room on a busy street or sidewalk. If only street-facing rooms are available, ask for one that isn't on the first floor.

2. Be sure they have an elevator so you don't have to schlep your luggage up the stairs or if walking up stairs is hard for you. But remember: While a room that's close to the elevator can be convenient in some respects, a room that's too close to the elevator also can be noisy. The same is true for rooms next to the ice machine and/or vending machines, stairwells, ballrooms, bars, kitchens or outdoor ventilation systems for the hotel.

3. In Europe in particular, always ask to see the room before you put money down on it.

4. For that matter, ask to see two rooms. One might be a lot bigger or obviously better than the other.

5. If something just doesn't suit you, don't be afraid to make an alternate reservation.

Get it in writing — yours and theirs

Be sure you write down all your reservation information when booking accommodations. Who did you talk to? When did you talk to them? Confirmation number. The price, including the tax. And not just the sales tax. Many cities pay for things like football and baseball stadiums by tacking on the tax to your hotel bill. This is known as an "occupancy tax," and there's not much you can do about it, but you should at least know what it's going to cost you ahead of time.

Don't just write the information down yourself, though. Get it in writing from the hotel. Have them mail, e-mail or fax you all of your reservation/confirmation info. In the event that there are any problems with your reservation when you arrive, it's not just your word against theirs. You'll be armed with documentation on the hotel's letterhead.

Tips for getting the best rate

The standard travel tip disclaimer applies here. These are guidelines, often true, subject to exceptions, but always worth considering:

• Call hotels directly to get a better deal. Don't call national toll-free numbers. If you call the toll-free number, you're talking to an operator that may be hundreds of miles from where you want to stay. Call the hotel property, ask for the manager on duty, and often they'll give you a better rate.

• Use every discount you have and never be afraid to ask. If you're a senior, ask if they have a senior discount. If you're traveling with children, ask if kids stay and eat free or at a discounted rate. Many hotels have family plans, adjoining rooms and no charge for children 17 and under. Ask!

• If you're a AAA member, let them know. Check to see if they have a AAA member discount. Many hotels and inns offer a discount for AAA members. Ask when you make your reservation. Show your AAA card when you check in and out. Make sure you get your discount if they offer one.

• Hotels near airports and train stations almost always are more expensive. Same story with downtown hotels. If the convenience is worth it to you, no problem. Otherwise, you can save money by staying in less-centralized locations.

• Earn frequent flyer miles when staying in hotels. Pay with a frequent flyer credit card. Also, double up on your discounts whenever possible. For example, pay with a credit card that earns frequent flyer miles when staying in a hotel that gives a discount to AAA members.

- Don't be afraid to barter. Room rates can be surprisingly negotiable. It's that same old supply side economics principle at work: The less demand there is for rooms, the more flexible the rates are. For example, if accommodations are readily available elsewhere and you show up late one night at a hotel that's nowhere near full, see if you can get them to knock the price down. You'd be surprised how often this works. Make an offer; see what they say.

- The best time to get a great deal when making a reservation is late Sunday afternoon. Most hotels are just trying to fill rooms at this point, and you're more likely to get a cheaper rate than if you call on a Friday.

- As with all things travel, the off-season is cheaper for hotel rates in most places.

- National and city tourist offices can help you find less-expensive lodgings. They can supply you lists of bargain hotels, hostels and people who rent rooms at reasonable rates.

Just the fax, ma'am, just the fax

Many hotels in the world don't have e-mail and are not ideal to contact by phone because of language barriers and expensive international long-distance rates. Try faxing instead. When making hotel reservations for a trip I took to Prague a few years ago, I faxed hotels directly before I left home. You can get hotel fax numbers from guidebooks or The OAG Travel Planner, a reference book where you can find telephone numbers, toll-free numbers, fax numbers and addresses for hotels all over the world. (Ask your travel agent — most use it as a reference.)

Rather than spending time and money trying to explain my accommodation needs to a hotel clerk who spoke very little English, I just faxed Prague in the evening, my time. I didn't have to think about the time difference, and it was cheap for me to do on my fax machine. I just typed out "I need a hotel room, this night, how much?" They faxed me back within a couple of hours with price and availability information. The advantage of this system is that you also get written confirmation of your reservations right away.

Meals and deals

Many accommodations offer meal options and/or cooking facilities that will save you money. Eating at restaurants can eat up your travel budget in no time. Here are some tips for eating well on the cheap — and some common meal plan terms explained:

- A lot of hotels have complimentary breakfast or a continental breakfast. Check to see if yours does before you make your reservation. That's one less meal a day to buy in a restaurant, and it can add up to big savings.

- Even if a continental breakfast isn't included in the price, many hotels supply a coffeepot and coffee in the room. Add some fruit and/or a few breakfast bars from the store, and you're good to go.

- If you're vacationing in one spot for a while — especially if you're with your family — consider getting a room with a full kitchen or at least a partial kitchen (sink, refrigerator, microwave). Buying groceries and doing your own cooking (or making lunches for the day) can save lots of money.

A glossary of meal plans from around the world

You get what you pay for, but what exactly are you paying for?

The American plan

Full breakfast, lunch and dinner included in the price of your room.

Pay first; you'll completely enjoy yourself later

Go all inclusive! When you book a "standard package" that includes hotel, transfers and taxes, one of two things will probably happen: Either you spend more money than you planned on or you don't do the things you wanted to do because prices are higher than you thought.

When your holiday is prepaid, you'll take that fishing trip on the safari, you'll windsurf, you'll go parasailing, and you'll eat until you're stuffed. In other words, you'll completely enjoy yourself.

Kelly Brock
AAA Travel Consultant
Bluffton, S.C.

Continental breakfast

- In North America, this is a breakfast buffet — but usually not a full bacon-and-eggs type breakfast: juice, coffee, milk, cereal, bagels, muffins, toast, fruit.
- In Great Britain, it usually means every imaginable breakfast food, cooked and otherwise. Hail, Britannia!
- In continental Europe, it's coffee and hot milk, jam, butter and a roll.

Modified American plan (or MAP)

The American plan on a budget. Breakfast only, included with the price of your room.

MAKING YOUR STAY MORE PLEASANT

Noise, street lights, unreliable wake-up calls, pillows the size of a big sack of potatoes seemingly designed by the Neck-Kinks-Are-Us Pillow Co. Little things can make a big difference, such as the difference between a bad night and a good one. You can't guarantee that the hotel will do right by you, but the prepared traveler can make it right. These portable items, useful in numerous travel situations, can greatly improve accommodations that aren't, well, as *accommodating* as they could be.

Why flip-flops are your friend

Let us now sing the praises of cheap, plastic flip-flops (or sandals). I've stayed in many lovely, inexpensive accommodations (especially in Europe) that had a shared bath down the hall. I always look to see what kind of condition the shared bathroom is in before I check in and pay for the room. Even so, I've never gotten comfortable with the idea of going barefoot in common baths and showers for any number of reasons that I'm sure don't need further explanation.

The solution? You guessed it: flip-flops. The cheaper the better — well, as long as the tread is good enough to keep you from slipping on the tile. The cheap ones are light, waterproof and plastic, perfect for slipping on your feet, padding down the hall and even showering in. They're easy to rinse off, quick to dry, and you can store them in a resealable plastic bag. They're perfect for beach vacations, too.

A great use for hotel shower caps

 Here's a nifty tip a clever traveler shared with me not long ago. Most hotel bathrooms come equipped with an elasticized plastic shower cap or two. These just happen to be dandy items for packing your shoes without soiling other items in your bag. Fast, effective and cheap. Just slip one over the bottom of each shoe and — *voila!* — the perfect packing solution for shoes. For more packing techniques and tips, see Chapters 7 and 8.

Rubber doorstop

A terrific, inexpensive, portable security system for hotel room doors. Always use the chain in addition to the deadbolt whenever it's available. But a little wedge-shaped rubber doorstop is a very effective item for increasing your hotel room's security.

Rubber sink plug

Particularly handy for the international traveler. Many rooms in the world don't have their own bathroom but do have a sink, although it's amazing how many sinks don't have adequate plugs for filling the basin when you want to wash, shave or rinse out a pair of socks. A tapered rubber sink plug can save the day.

Sleep mask

Too much street light? Inadequate blinds or curtains in your room? Two words: sleep mask. Bring one with you wherever you travel. (Ideal for sleeping on planes and trains, too.)

Earplugs

Earplugs are a very inexpensive way to shut out unwanted noise so you can sleep. A few words of caution: I recommend bringing several pairs and tossing them before they get grubby. Also, you want to make sure it's safe to use them. They block out noise, but some noises you need to hear, such as smoke alarms, intruders, etc. That's the cautious perspective. I love earplugs, but use them at your own discretion.

Travel alarm clock

A good backup system for wake-up calls — which usually are made when you requested them to be, but sometimes aren't.

Portable reading light

The quality of bedside lights in hotels around the world varies. Inexpensive, battery-powered, portable reading lights are a great way to compensate for inadequate light or to keep reading when your traveling companion wants to sleep or you want to check a map in the car.

Portable smoke alarm

Most rooms have smoke alarms. In some of the world's more exotic locations... well, let's just say they're not always a priority. Many travel stores sell portable smoke alarms you can put on the nightstand if you're concerned for your safety.

Inflatable neck pillow

This is another essential travel item — especially for long plane and train trips — that can substitute for an uncomfortable hotel pillow in a pinch.

CHAPTER 5

MONEY

*Means and methods of payment
(and how to protect them)*

METHODS OF PAYMENT

Multiply and conquer

Cash. Credit cards. ATM cards. Traveler's checks. Today's traveler has many methods of payment to choose from. But which one should you use? Answer: all of them. Never rely on just one method.

Why?

Because every method of payment has its advantages and its drawbacks. Having a variety of options maximizes your flexibility and assures that you're covered for nearly any contingency. I always have $75-$100 worth of cash in whatever the local currency is when I travel. I keep at least 10 U.S. $1 bills in my pocket and an ATM card, two credit cards and traveler's checks in my money belt.

In this chapter, we'll look at why you should have all of these methods of payment with you when you travel, the pros and cons of each method and which ones work best in specific situations. Let's start with the different options.

Cash

Cash is a necessity for all travelers. Don't assume you'll be able to find an ATM wherever you are. Always bring $75 to $100 worth of the local currency with you in case you need to catch a cab or get a room for the night and don't have fast access to a bank or a cash machine.

☑ *Methods of payment*

Make sure you bring the following methods of payment with you:

- ☐ $75-$100 worth of local currency
- ☐ 20 U.S. $1 bills
- ☐ ATM card
- ☐ Two credit cards
- ☐ Traveler's checks

It's always good to have cash as a backup system for your credit cards and traveler's checks. There are three key things you need to know about traveling with cash:

1. Where to carry it.
2. Don't carry too much of it.
3. Don't flash large amounts of it around in the open.

I rarely travel with more than $200 worth of cash in my possession. It's just not necessary to carry more than that in most situations, but I always keep it in my money belt if I do. The $75-$100 of local currency stays in my day bag where it's readily accessible and I can do things such as buy a sandwich or pay for cab fare without advertising to the world that I'm wearing a money belt. When you do need to access your money belt, there are ways to be discreet: in your hotel room, in the bathroom stall, in the privacy of a train compartment are examples.

As for the spending money you carry in your day bag (or your pocket), I recommend having it all in small denominations. This makes it easier to pay for small items along the way, tip with ease and minimize the hassle of too much change or being shortchanged if you can't instantly figure the conversion rate in your head. (What are the ideal items to pack in your walking-around day bag? Read Chapter 8, Packing, Stage Two.)

Credit cards

I travel with two credit cards at all times. Why two? Credit cards are incredibly convenient, but if you only bring one and it gets lost, stolen or stuck in an ATM machine, it can put you in a bind. Bring two. And keep them in your money belt.

Get a money belt/security wallet

This may be the most important tip in the whole chapter. There's no point in having access to multiple methods of payment if you don't protect them adequately. Money belts are absolutely the best way to make sure your cash, credit cards and traveler's checks don't get lost or stolen. For more information about money belts and a complete checklist of what items you should carry in them, see Chapter 8, Packing, Stage Two.

Credit card advantages

When it comes to budgeting and paying for your trip, getting good discounts and exchange rates, credit cards still reign. I'm not advocating racking up a huge bill on your credit card and letting it sit there, because with the interest you'll pay, there's no benefit.

But if you're able to start planning and saving up money for your trip before you go, you can use your credit cards to pay for nearly everything while you're on the road — your hotel bill, your plane tickets, shopping sprees. Then pay off the bill with your savings after you return. This way you get all of the advantages of credit cards (frequent flyer miles, the best exchange rates, not having to carry lots of cash) without the disadvantages of being in debt and paying interest on a big balance).

Here are some tips about credit cards:

• When traveling in foreign countries, put your hotel expenses on a credit card so you get the best exchange rate.

• Use credit cards that give you some kind of benefit,
  especially frequent flyer miles.

• Be careful with the receipts. Don't let your credit card numbers fall into the wrong hands. Keep your receipts for your records or dispose of them in a way that no one can find them and get your card number.

• Make a list of all your credit card (and traveler's check numbers, too, while you're at it) and toll-free customer service numbers in case your card is lost or stolen. Keep a copy with you and leave a copy with a trusted contact at home. This makes it easy to report a missing card and to get it replaced as soon as possible.

• Know your pin number. In Europe, they don't use letters on the ATM machine key pads.

Traveler's checks

Some people think that credit cards and ATM cards have replaced the need for traveler's checks. Not true. Credit cards and ATM cards are a tremendous convenience, but cash machines aren't always readily available internationally. Sometimes they eat your card, and sometimes cards get refused because of a technical glitch somewhere in the system. These may be exceptions to the rule, but they do happen. And if they happen to you, you'll rejoice in the low-tech simplicity of the traveler's check.

As for cash, if it's lost or stolen, it's gone for good. Traveler's checks are the best backup plan you can have. They're an insurance policy on your money. If they're lost or stolen, they can be replaced by American Express® usually within 24 hours. (I use them as an example because I use their traveler's checks — or "cheques" as they call them.)

I discourage you from carrying a lot of cash on your trip, unless you're going someplace so remote or exotic that it's the only accepted method of payment. In many adventure travel destinations and in places such as Eastern Europe, traveler's checks aren't always accepted. In the world's most far-flung corners, commerce operates on an exclusive cash-and-carry basis. If you're doing exotic travel, check with your travel agent before you go and find out if the locals take credit cards or traveler's checks before you show up assuming they do.

Tips for using traveler's checks

- The best place to cash a traveler's check without being charged a fee is at the traveler's check office. Ask for a list of their offices throughout the world. Or ask at a local bank to see if they charge a fee.

- Don't cash them at the hotel or in a boutique, because they'll almost always take a bigger exchange rate.

- A good travel agent will be able to give you a list of places at your destination where you can cash traveler's checks without paying a fee.

- If you're traveling as a couple, get dual-signature traveler's checks so either one of you can cash them without the other having to be there. This simple tip can make for a much more harmonious trip.

- Most traveler's check issuers level a 1 percent to 2 percent fee on the amount you purchase. AAA members can get traveler's checks from AAA Travel Agencies without having to pay a fee.

Stored value cards: payment solutions

 Stored value cards offer convenience, security, flexibility and favorable currency exchange rates. Each stored value card is a prepaid credit card that holds a prepaid dollar amount established by you beforehand. As you use it, the amount you spend is deducted from the total. There's no waiting for check approval or having to carry lots of cash. Stored value cards are a great way to budget your spending and maximize your secure payment options around the world.

Tip-money and the all-purpose dollar bill

Have tip money ready, in your pocket, in small denominations. You should always tip in the currency of the country you're traveling in. But you may not always have the local currency handy. That's why I suggest keeping at least 10 U.S. $1 bills accessible in your pocket or day bag. They're accepted as tips nearly everywhere, and most of the world still loves the U.S. dollar because it's a hard, stable currency. And remember: small bills — in any currency — are preferable because, as a rule, when you tip, you don't want to ask for change if you can help it. For more information on the delicate art of tipping around the world, see Chapter 19, Tips on Tipping.

• Keep two separate copies of your check numbers. Leave one at home with your contact person. If your checks are lost or stolen, this will make your life much easier — and check replacement much faster.

Tips for exchanging money and dealing with foreign currency

• Airports and train stations are just about the worst places you can change money. They really gouge you on the exchange rate.

• Plan ahead: It's best to order foreign currency from a bank at home before you go on your trip. Banks will give you a better rate, but you often have to order foreign currency a week or two in advance of when you need it unless you live in a big city. Leave yourself some time to do this, and you'll save money (and time spent waiting in lines when you're on vacation).

• Be sure you get foreign currency in advance for each country you're going to. Keep different currencies separate from one another. Small resealable plastic bags are a great way to do this. Otherwise things can get confusing fast. You want to be neat and organized. Individual plastic bags are the way to go.

• I also love the coin purses you see all over Europe. People over there are so used to dealing with lots of different currencies that you'll see these great coin purses with different pockets and different colored zippers to keep track of the different currencies. A handy item to have when you're traveling through five countries in Europe in the course of two weeks.

- Bring a credit-card-size, solar-powered calculator. They're very handy for doing conversions and calculating exchange rates in a hurry — and don't take up much space.

And, finally, save your receipts!

A good way to save your travel receipts is in plain manila envelopes: 8 ½ x 11 or regular letter-size envelopes individually marked for each country you're traveling through. Keep them organized and bring some paper clips with you. Why should travelers save their receipts?

- For customs (more on this later).

- To calculate the exchange rate/keep track of the amount withdrawn in a foreign currency when your bank statement comes.

- To keep your credit card numbers out of the hands of would-be frauds.

- In some countries like Canada, you can turn in your receipts (above a certain dollar amount) and get money back. Check at duty-free shops to see the latest rates and refund terms.

Spare change and what to do with it when you get home

Many are the world travelers who come home from a European vacation with 5 pounds worth of spare change in seven different currencies weighing down their pockets. Total street value: $7.52. What should you do with this change? Let's be franc, whoops, I mean *frank*: You should keep it moving.

Tip: Many airlines will collect coins for charities. Cruise ships will do this, too. This can be a good way to put your spare currency change to good use. Coins also can make nice souvenirs or small gifts for kids or grandkids (as long as they're past the coin-swallowing stage of childhood development). Or you can do the decent thing and simply buy as much chocolate as you possibly can at the duty-free shop. We all have our favorite causes.

Mini-checklist of things you can spend your spare change on:

- Charity donation
- Magazines
- Gifts
- Chocolate (personal charity)
- Fountains/wishes

When traveling internationally

1. Beware of exchange bureaus that offer extremely low exchange rates. They may have high service charges to make up for the difference.

2. Compare rates when exchanging money — commissions very greatly from place to place.

3. Before entering another country, get the next country's currency. If you arrive in the next country at night or on a holiday, you might not be able to get money at a bank, currency exchange or store.

4. Banks usually have the best exchange rates and the lowest fees. The bigger the bank, the better.

5. Try to exchange larger amounts of money less frequently, rather than exchanging small amounts more frequently.

6. Beware of black market money exchanges — you may receive bills that are counterfeit or out of circulation.

7. Be cautious of local residents who claim they can give you an excellent personal exchange rate. You may be setting yourself up for a robbery.

8. Consider using your ATM card to obtain cash, rather than paying high service charges.

9. Take only those credit cards you plan on using. Leave other cards at home in a secure place. Credit cards provide a record of purchases and are good to have when an unexpected expense or emergency comes about.

10. Credit card charges in a foreign currency are usually converted at either the wholesale market rate or a government-mandated rate in effect one day prior to the processing date, increased by 1 percent, which the credit card company retains as compensation for the conversion service.

Gary A. Kraft, CTC
AAA Group Travel Services Director
Bettendorf, Iowa

CHAPTER 6

PAPERWORK, IDENTIFICATION AND IMPORTANT DOCUMENTS

*What you'll need,
when you'll need it,
where you'll need it*

Travel, and especially international travel, requires a number of crucial pieces of paper. Here are some that you may need for your trip.

PASSPORTS

Your passport is your entrée into nearly every country on the planet. And for international travelers, it's by far the most important piece of paper you'll carry with you on your trip. Treat it with respect. Develop a healthy sense of reverence for your passport, and you'll never be completely helpless, even if your luggage, cash and sense of well-being travel on without you for some reason.

Getting a passport is easy but time-consuming, unless you're willing to pay extra fees to expedite the process. First, you need to get the  correct passport application, which can be found at any passport acceptance facility: your local post office, a municipal office, courthouse or library. Most travel agents keep applications on hand as well. But here's a timesaving tip: You can get a head start by downloading the correct application from the State Department's website at state.gov. This website also can be used to locate the passport facility nearest you by city or zip code.

If you're applying for your first passport, you have to make a personal appearance at the passport facility with your completed application, two regulation 2-inch-by-2-inch photos of yourself and proof of your citizenship. (A birth certificate is preferable for proving your citizenship, but there's an exhaustive list of alternatives listed on the aforementioned State Department site.) If you're replacing an expired passport, you can use that as your identification to get a new one. If you're renewing a current passport (or replacing one that expired less than 12 years ago), you can send it along with your completed application, photos and fee to the address on the application, and you'll receive a new passport through the mail.

The normal processing time to obtain a passport is six weeks, but it can take as long as three months during peak travel times when demand is high. Needless to say, you want to start early. If your itinerary includes countries that require visas, you should start the passport acquisition process six months in advance of your trip to allow for the back-and-forth mailing of your documents. (See *Visas* on the next page.) The current cost of a passport for travelers 14 years and older is $60, and $40 for people renewing a current passport or for anyone under 14 years of age.

To be safe when traveling internationally

When traveling outside the United States, be sure to carry **a copy** of your passport in your luggage, but not in the same bag that your original passport is in.

Boo Ring
AAA Manager
Bluffton, S.C.

If you need your passport in a hurry, there are other options and, naturally, they cost more. But not ridiculously more. If you live near a major city that has a passport agency, it's possible to get a passport in as little as two weeks for an extra $35. Passport agencies generally operate by appointment only and most likely will ask to see proof of your imminent departure, such as an airline ticket or itinerary. If you're really in a bind, there's no shortage of free-lance passport expediting services (online and in the phone book) that promise to get your passport to you in as little as 24 hours for an additional charge. These services aren't cheap, and it's preferable to use them only if you're really in a jam.

Common-sense travel tip: Get at least six extra copies of your passport photos. If your passport is lost or stolen, the last thing you want to deal with is getting your picture taken. Also, if you're traveling to any countries that require a visa, you'll need more photos.

VISAS

Visas are sort of like filters countries put up to screen visitors. A visa is a document (or, in many cases, a stamp in your passport) issued by a country that requires its permission for you to enter. Visas generally are good for very specific, limited periods of time, and the requirements for any given country can change frequently due to shifting political climates and security issues. These requirements can, and often do, favor citizens of particular countries over others.

Since it's generally much easier to obtain a visa before you travel to your destination, the best thing to do is to consult individual embassies or consulates for their current policies before you leave. Online, go to embassyworld.com for locations of foreign embassies and consulates in the United States and abroad.

To get a visa, you must get an application directly from the closest consulate or embassy of the country you wish to visit, either in person or by mail. You then submit your passport along with the completed application and fee, and then wait for your passport to come back with

 the visa. Some visas require extra passport pictures, and most applications will ask you to state your purpose for visiting. Usually they want to know whether you're a tourist, a student or traveling on business. Remember that when you apply for a visa (and send your passport in with the application), you're at the mercy of a foreign bureaucracy. There are no guarantees when it comes to timing. It could take *weeks* to get your passport back, which is another good reason to start the entire process months in advance.

Common-sense travel tip: You can get a visa while you're traveling, but you may be delayed for unpredictable periods of time in a foreign city. It's better and sometimes necessary to obtain a visa *before* you travel.

IDENTIFICATION FOR THE PLANE

Whether you're flying inside your home country or internationally, you'll need to present photo identification every time you check in for your flight (and sometimes again before you board the plane). A driver's license is the most commonly used form of photo ID. But if you don't drive, your passport is an acceptable alternative to your driver's license. If you don't have a driver's license or a passport, you still can get a personal photo ID issued from the Department of Licensing in your home state. It looks like a driver's license but is for identification purposes only. Whichever method you use, be absolutely sure you bring some (legal) form of photo ID with you when you fly. You will be denied boarding without it.

INTERNATIONAL DRIVING PERMIT

If you plan to drive overseas to a country where English is not the primary language, an International Driving Permit or Inter-American Driving Permit is a useful secondary form of identification to have with you. An IDP (or IADP) is a document that translates your name and driving information into 10 different languages and is valid in 150 different countries. Although you can get by in western Europe (except for Spain) with your state driver's license, many experienced travelers recommend carrying an IDP, even if you're not going to be behind the wheel.

Getting an IDP isn't like getting a regular driver's license. There's no test to take, it's good for one year, and it's easily obtained from your local AAA office for about $10, even if you aren't a AAA member. Just supply your valid driver's license and two passport-size photos (you can have your picture taken on the premises), and AAA will give you the IDP application form to fill out. Or you can visit aaa.com for information on how to download the application and complete the entire transaction by mail.

IMMUNIZATIONS AND VACCINATIONS

Some countries require proof of vaccination against certain diseases, such as yellow fever and malaria, before they'll allow you to cross their borders. No less than 40 countries currently require proof of an HIV test. Before you leave, consult the Centers for Disease Control website at cdc.gov for the latest alerts. The CDC provides information about outbreaks of disease around the world and makes recommendations for immunizations.

You also can order an International Certificate of Vaccination from CDC's website. This is an internationally recognized document that proves you've taken necessary medical precautions. It's basically just a list of vaccinations that your doctor can sign and date to verify that you've had the necessary shots. It's small enough to keep in your passport (which is a good place for it). Even if you aren't traveling down the Amazon, it's a good idea to update vaccinations. Be sure to leave a copy of this document at home with someone who can fax it to you if you lose it.

Plan on and purchase travel insurance

1. Buy cancellation insurance to protect your investment.
2. Make sure your health insurance covers you when you travel abroad. If not, buy health insurance, too.
3. If you rent a car, check with your credit card company to see if they offer coverage.
4. Ensure that you get coverage information in writing, and review it so you know what the deductibles are.
5. Also check the car rental company to see if they offer coverage. Find out the cost of "loss of use" insurance.

Susan Ledford
AAA General Manager
Hendersonville Service Office, N.C.

PRESCRIPTIONS AND MEDICATIONS

If you have a pre-existing medical condition that requires special treatment, bring along documentation from your doctor explaining your condition, along with your doctor's name, phone number and address. If you're ever in a position where you're unable to communicate easily, you'll want to have this information with you. Even if you don't have any chronic conditions that need treatment, carry information about your blood type and allergies just in case you need it.

INSURANCE POLICIES

Auto insurance, trip insurance, medical insurance: Throughout this book, we'll talk about different insurance options for travelers. But whatever coverage you choose to have for your trip, make sure to bring your policy information and insurance cards with you, including contact numbers for your insurance agent and travel agent. Should you have to use your insurance for any reason, you'll need to have that information handy. Insurance policies vary. Don't assume yours covers you no matter where you go. Consult your agent before traveling overseas. Find out the exact terms of your coverage before you go.

CHILD CUSTODY DOCUMENTATION

This is a relatively new aspect of international travel. Single parents, grandparents and/or guardians who are traveling with children need to be prepared to prove that they're doing so legally, with the full consent of *both* the child's parents. Canada, in particular, is quite vigilant about this. Here's an excerpt from a State Department Consular Information Sheet on Canada:

> Pease note that due to international concern over child abduction, single parents, grandparents or guardians traveling with children often need proof of custody or notarized letters from the other parent authorizing travel. Anyone under age 18 and traveling alone should carry a letter from his/her parent or guardian authorizing the trip.

Canada is not alone in its concern. Mexico also requires notarized consent from a parent for any child traveling alone, with one parent or with a guardian. When in doubt, check the State Department's listings of foreign entry requirements. Even if you don't need a notarized letter of authorization for a country, it's a good idea to have at least the child's birth certificate documenting you as the birth parent and/or a signed letter from the child's other parent. Single parents, grandparents or guardians may want to have a notarized letter with them to prevent any possible misunderstandings at a border crossing.

CHAPTER 7

PACKING, STAGE ONE

*Packing principles, checklists galore
and more than a few tips to help
take the 'lug' out of luggage*

LIGHTEN UP!
Guiding philosophies and packing principles

I believe in packing light — as light as you possibly can and still have everything you need. As a student some 20 years ago, I lived and traveled in Europe for many months. One of the most important lessons I learned from personal observation was that while Americans feel the need to carry everything with them, Europeans don't. Back then, my fellow students and I were schlepping way too much luggage on and off trains and everywhere we went. It was a real hindrance to our mobility, and it was exhausting. I'd see European travelers from all over the continent traveling comfortably with one or two little bags. The nickel finally dropped. I thought: Obviously there's a better way to do this.

And so there is. When you're trying to get away from it all, don't take it all with you. Take what you need. I realize that travelers have their own opinion of what they need. For those of you who don't share my philosophy of traveling light, well, you can always bring more stuff if you want to. But I do think it's helpful to at least know *how* to bring less.

Things <u>not</u> to pack

1. Too many shoes. Limit yourself to three pairs — including the ones you'll wear in transit.
2. Too much paper. Paper is heavy. Only bring the reading material you really need and/or can use. This is especially true of travel guides, phrase books and maps. Before you go, narrow them down to the ones you really need for your destination.
3. Home-sized toiletries. Use samples or travel-sized toiletries to save weight and space.
4. Never pack anything of value in checked luggage including money, cameras, medicine, expensive jewelry, traveler's checks, travel documents — including your airline ticket — matches, cigarette lighters, butane for curling irons. Ask your travel agent if you are unsure about any other items.
5. Anything you'd really hate to lose, that has sentimental value or is otherwise irreplaceable.

NOTE TO READER

Checklists are carved from experience, not stone

The checklists in this chapter (and the next one) are my opinion of what works best — for me and, hopefully, for you, too. But checklists are sort of like recipes in a cookbook. You can follow them to the letter, or you can adapt them to fit your individual tastes for travel. If nothing else, I hope these checklists will remind you of something you otherwise might have forgotten or simply wouldn't have thought of in the first place.

As many years as I've traveled, as many trips as I've taken, I'm still learning new and better ways to travel all the time, with every trip I take. I encourage you to think of travel as an education that's never really finished. There's never a point at which we travelers get a diploma informing us that we've graduated. If travel experience is the best teacher — and I think it is — it's a teacher that never stops teaching, unless you stop traveling. But who would want to do that?

Not me. So, yes, these packing lists and tips are based on my experiences. Feel free to treat them as gospel truth or very rough guidelines that you can follow or adapt to the extent you wish.

One of the best things about travel is the people you meet and the things you learn from one another. Talking to people is one of the best ways I know to learn about travel. Sure, when it comes to other people's opinions, you have to sort out what you take with a grain of salt and what you think is valuable information or at least information that's applicable to you. But that's true of anything in life. Trust your best instincts, no matter whose opinion you're taking — or leaving, as the case may be.

That said, when it comes to packing, here's my opinion of what you should take, what you should leave and how to decide that.

Follow this formula

When traveling, take half the clothes, twice as much money and three times the photographic film you think you will need.

Peggy Chestnut
AAA Leisure Travel Agent
Myrtle Beach, S.C.

YOUR TRAVEL WARDROBE
Pick basic colors

Choosing a travel wardrobe of basic colors will help you deal with space limitations. Build your wardrobe using one or two basic colors, so that the same shoes, hosiery and accessories can be worn with pretty much everything. Some versatile color combinations are black and red, navy and red, brown and beige or black and white. Simple, classic styles for dress and casual wear work best. Make sure each item of clothing can be worn in at least two different outfits.

Pack to match your destination's climate

For warmer climates, pack lighter colors and natural fabrics, such as cotton. Unlike synthetics, cotton breathes. For cooler climates, dark-colored clothing, which can be layered for warmth, is a good choice. Wool gabardine is a good fabric to travel with, as it's lightweight, warm and wrinkle-resistant.

One thing many travelers forget is that you're already wearing a day's outfit in addition to all the clothes already packed, so don't duplicate unnecessarily. For in-transit outfits, go with loose-fitting clothing with elastic waistbands and comfortable shoes for walking long distances in airports and train stations.

Keep track of what you pack

Organizing your wardrobe is easier if you have a list of things that you plan to take with you. Keep the list of items in your carry-on bag. If checked bags are misplaced, the list of contents can help identify them.

When packing for kids

A great idea when packing children's clothing is to put an entire day's outfit (including underwear and socks) in a large resealable plastic bag and write the child's name on the outside of the bag. This can be particularly helpful when traveling with more than one child, and it saves time spent searching through luggage for individual items.

PACKING LISTS
His, hers and theirs

Here are some checklists for any combination of travelers, for weekend getaways or longer stays.

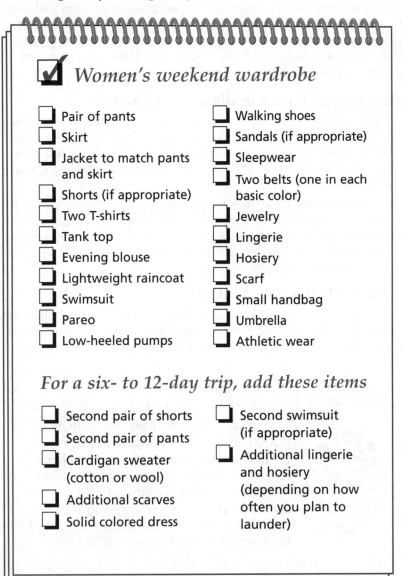

☑ *Women's weekend wardrobe*

- Pair of pants
- Skirt
- Jacket to match pants and skirt
- Shorts (if appropriate)
- Two T-shirts
- Tank top
- Evening blouse
- Lightweight raincoat
- Swimsuit
- Pareo
- Low-heeled pumps
- Walking shoes
- Sandals (if appropriate)
- Sleepwear
- Two belts (one in each basic color)
- Jewelry
- Lingerie
- Hosiery
- Scarf
- Small handbag
- Umbrella
- Athletic wear

For a six- to 12-day trip, add these items

- Second pair of shorts
- Second pair of pants
- Cardigan sweater (cotton or wool)
- Additional scarves
- Solid colored dress
- Second swimsuit (if appropriate)
- Additional lingerie and hosiery (depending on how often you plan to launder)

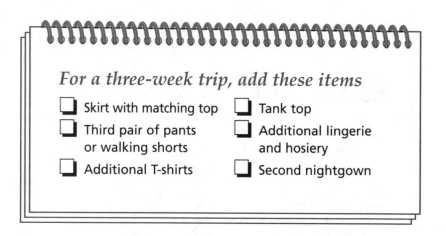

For a three-week trip, add these items

- ☐ Skirt with matching top
- ☐ Third pair of pants or walking shorts
- ☐ Additional T-shirts
- ☐ Tank top
- ☐ Additional lingerie and hosiery
- ☐ Second nightgown

Cultural differences and 'convertible' pant legs

 Men and women (and especially women, I'm afraid) always have to consider cultural differences when packing for certain destinations. There are a number of places in the world where people are offended by the sight of other people wearing shorts. Your response to this — indifference, rebellion or flexibility (I recommend the latter, as it's less hassle and you get to see more of the world) — is up to you, but you always should consider carefully before you go. Even in parts of the world where it's not normally an issue (most of Europe, for example), you often encounter restrictions in cathedrals and specific destinations such as the Vatican. Plan accordingly.

One way of dealing with this situation is to purchase a pair of pants with "convertible" legs — that is, legs that can be zipped off and zipped back on to convert them from long pants to shorts as circumstances (including fluctuating temperatures) require. You can find pants with convertible legs in nearly every good travel and outdoor outfitting catalog and store. It's also a good idea for women to bring a comfortable travel dress with a low hemline (that is, below the knee).

For more on cultural differences and how to deal with them gracefully, see Chapter 24, Cultural Considerations.

☑ Men's weekend wardrobe

- ☐ Casual slacks (the color khaki goes with almost anything and hides dirt well)
- ☐ Dress slacks
- ☐ Jacket that coordinates with both slacks
- ☐ Tie (if appropriate)
- ☐ Two short-sleeved shirts (one polo and one T-shirt)
- ☐ Long-sleeved shirt
- ☐ Sweater
- ☐ Shorts

- ☐ Swim trunks
- ☐ Two belts
- ☐ Undershorts
- ☐ Undershirts
- ☐ Casual socks
- ☐ Sleepwear
- ☐ Casual shoes
- ☐ Flip-flops or sandals
- ☐ Dress shoes and socks (if appropriate)
- ☐ Lightweight overcoat
- ☐ Umbrella
- ☐ Athletic wear

For a six- to 12-day trip, add these items

- ☐ A suit (dark for formal occasions)
- ☐ V-neck or crew-neck sweater with coordinating slacks

- ☐ Additional shorts
- ☐ Additional undershorts and undershirts
- ☐ Additional socks

For a three-week trip, add these items

- ☐ Casual pants
- ☐ Sweatpants and sweatshirt (neutral color)
- ☐ Additional tie

- ☐ Additional underwear
- ☐ Additional shirts

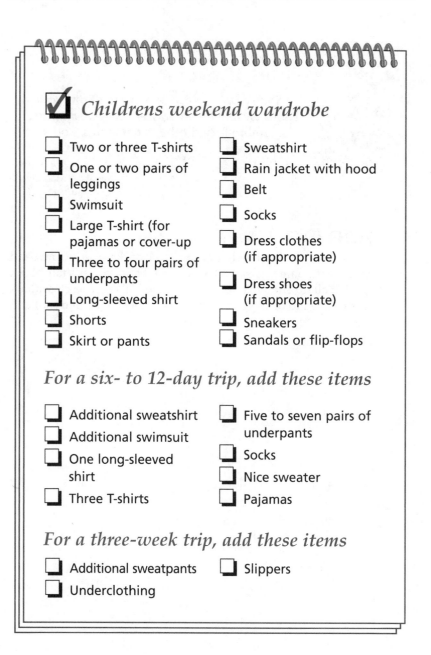

✓ Childrens weekend wardrobe

- ☐ Two or three T-shirts
- ☐ One or two pairs of leggings
- ☐ Swimsuit
- ☐ Large T-shirt (for pajamas or cover-up)
- ☐ Three to four pairs of underpants
- ☐ Long-sleeved shirt
- ☐ Shorts
- ☐ Skirt or pants

- ☐ Sweatshirt
- ☐ Rain jacket with hood
- ☐ Belt
- ☐ Socks
- ☐ Dress clothes (if appropriate)
- ☐ Dress shoes (if appropriate)
- ☐ Sneakers
- ☐ Sandals or flip-flops

For a six- to 12-day trip, add these items

- ☐ Additional sweatshirt
- ☐ Additional swimsuit
- ☐ One long-sleeved shirt
- ☐ Three T-shirts

- ☐ Five to seven pairs of underpants
- ☐ Socks
- ☐ Nice sweater
- ☐ Pajamas

For a three-week trip, add these items

- ☐ Additional sweatpants
- ☐ Underclothing

- ☐ Slippers

Stuff 'em with lots of small stuff

 Shoes. Don't leave 'em empty! Stuff your shoes with underwear, scarves, jewelry, purse-size umbrella and other small items. You'll save space.

Boo Ring
AAA Manager
Bluffton, S.C.

READY TO PACK IT UP?

Now that we've discussed some general packing principles and considered the fundamentals of what you need to pack, let's talk about how to pack it all up and what to pack it in. We'll also take a closer look at what items need to be in your carry-on bag, day bag, toiletry kit and money belt.

Let's get packing.

CHAPTER 8

PACKING, STAGE TWO

How to pack it, what to pack it in
and lots more packing tips
for every traveler (and most every bag)

IT'S NOT JUST WHAT GOES IN YOUR BAG...

It's how you put it in there. And this chapter covers both of these topics, with more specific tips and suggestions about how to pack and *what* to pack in your different bags. Detailed, individual checklists have been compiled at the end of the chapter so that if you care to use them as guidelines when you pack, you won't have to flip pages back and forth to do so. Where you see duplicate items on these lists, I'm not suggesting you double-pack them. I'm simply offering up different checklist-item groupings/categories to suit individual travelers. In addition to the checklists, I've also compiled some of my favorite packing-related tips toward the end of the chapter.

As you read this chapter, keep in mind, there's such a wide spectrum of travel these days, and, naturally, every traveler has to tailor his or her packing to fit specific travel needs. Many of us travel to the same destinations all over the world, but every traveler has individual requirements and preferences. So, again, I encourage you to amend checklists and suggestions to fit your particular situation and method of travel.

PACKING YOUR CARRY-ON BAG

If possible, try to travel with only carry-on-style luggage. If your bag is heavy and doesn't have wheels, you should borrow one with wheels or consider buying one. Wheeled luggage saves your shoulder and back muscles and keeps fatigue to a minimum. For smaller bags without wheels, pack only the items you feel you'll need in transit. However, any trip that will require a lot of walking is best done with wheeled luggage in tow.

Pack as many of your carry-on bag items as you can in resealable plastic bags. This makes it easier to find and identify your bag's contents, and when you pull them out, everything else doesn't fall to the bottom.

Most importantly, if you're traveling to a meeting or a special occasion and you need to be dressed appropriately, be sure to wear what you need or carry it on the plane with you. It's one less thing to worry about if you're separated from your luggage. And ...

When in doubt, leave it out!

Always call your airline before you go and find out what their carry-on restrictions are. Each airline has its own rules for how many bags you can carry on and what items should never be in your carry-on bag. Obviously, anything that could be used as a weapon is out of the question — scissors, pocketknives, knitting needles, etc. When in doubt, don't pack it in your carry-on bag.

In the meantime, I'm assuming the trend will be toward smaller carry-on bags in general. As of this writing, I doubt carry-on bags will be completely prohibited, but it's safe to say they will be scrutinized more than ever and that the limitations/rules will be much more rigidly enforced. We travelers have a responsibility to ourselves and to each other to be patient about the time and inconvenience this sometimes will entail.

Carry-on bag tips

• Put a collapsible tote bag inside your carry-on bag — something lightweight and very compact, with straps so you can just throw it over your shoulder. Should you have to check a bigger carry-on bag, you can pull out the essentials, put them in the tote and check the rest.

• I recommend carry-on bags with an outside pocket for your water bottle. This not only keeps your water easily accessible so you can stay hydrated when you fly (very important), but, should your water bottle leak or spill, it won't make a mess inside your bag.

• Expandable carry-on bags also are very helpful. We naturally tend to accumulate things as we travel — clothing, gifts, souvenirs and so on — and most travelers come home with more things than they left with. Plan ahead. With an expandable carry-on bag, you can make more room as you go, check the bag on the way home if you need to and put your essential carry-on items in the lightweight collapsible tote bag that you brought in your carry-on bag.

Before you begin your family vacation

Take a map of the state or region you'll be visiting and highlight the route you'll be taking. Tape the map on the wall at eye level for the kids. Cut out photos of grandma and grandpa or other family members you're visiting and tape the pictures near the spot on the map where they live and where you're going.

I did this for my nieces and it was quite a hit with them. We even added Rudolph at the North Pole and circled where their favorite animals live.

PACKING YOUR MAIN BAG

Maximize space and minimize wrinkles — seven easy steps

"Interlayering" is the name given to the following method of packing either soft or hard luggage. Not only can it save space, it's a great way to minimize wrinkles. Begin by opening your suitcase on a flat surface.

1. Place your shoes, in pairs, inside plastic bags. Configure them toe-to-heel or tuck one into the other, if possible, to maximize space. (A woman's size 8 slides neatly inside a man's loafer size 10.) Put your shoes and heavy items on the bottom (near the hinges, if you're using a hard-shell case). Place belts along the perimeter of the case, as well as heavy items like a hairdryer and cosmetic case.

2. Now place a divider on top of these items. If your suitcase doesn't come with a divider, you can make your own either by: folding a plastic dry-cleaner bag into thirds; using an oversized placemat; or cutting a piece of cardboard the size of your suitcase (with cutouts for your hands, to make it easier to lift out). Cover your divider with Con-Tact® paper to make it more durable.

3. Fold the slacks along their natural creases and place the waistband against one edge of your suitcase with the bottom of the pants extending over the opposite edge of the case. Using the same technique, place the second pair of slacks in the opposite direction.

4. Continue folding the skirts and dresses along their natural creases and use the interlayering technique of layering each article in the opposite direction until all your slacks, skirts and dresses are packed.

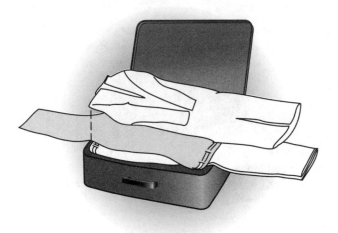

5. Next, button up all jackets and blazers and pull a dry-cleaner bag over them. (Note: Use dry-cleaner bags without print on them, as it may rub off in more humid climates.) Place them face-down in the suitcase with the sleeves being brought to the back of the jacket along their natural creases. The bottom of the jackets will extend over the top edge of the suitcase.

6. Roll up all knit items and place them on top of the layered clothing, leaving the original articles extended over the edges of the case. When you've utilized every inch of space, bring the ends over the rolled items inside the case, alternating sides as you go. This

keeps your clothing in a rounded shape, minimizing creases and wrinkles in the knee area of the slacks and on jacket waistlines. It's also easier to pull out certain items you may need along the way without disturbing the entire case full of clothes.

7. When all items are packed, you'll notice the great benefit of having the divider in the middle of the suitcase: You can reach in and lift out the entire top layer of your packed items without disturbing the items on top (also excellent for customs searches), and you can easily retrieve items from (or add items to) the bottom half of the suitcase.

Several smooth suggestions for thwarting wrinkles

• Stuff your shoes with socks, hose, underwear or anything else that either won't wrinkle easily or be seen if it does wrinkle.

• Place tissue paper between garment folds.

• To minimize wrinkles in pleated skirts, turn them inside out, wrap masking tape around the hem (to keep the pleats set), roll the skirt from the side to create a long "tube," and pull the skirt into an old pair of panty hose with the top and bottom cut off. This will keep the pleats in and the skirt from wrinkling. Place around the perimeter of your case.

• Roll your outfits together if they're knits. They won't wrinkle, and you won't have to search for all of your accessories. Add matching socks and underclothes.

• Wrap men's ties around a piece of cardboard and secure with a wide piece of elastic.

• Sweaters are easy to roll up, usually don't wrinkle easily and fit well into corners, keeping other items from shifting in your suitcase.

• Fold blouses and men's shirts inside out so the wrinkles are facing inside and are not so prominent.

Additional tips for packing your suitcase

• Turn all sequined items or embroidered clothes inside out and place them either in a plastic bag or pillowcase to minimize rubbing and loosening of sequins. (You'll also have your own pillowcase on your trip.)

• Use your evening bag to store your jewelry so you know exactly where it is and which outfit you plan to wear it with.

• Place the items you intend to use first on the top of your suitcase: shorts, bathing suit, pajamas, etc.

- The contents of a suitcase tend to settle, leaving more space for additional items — this is a good reason to pack at least a day before your departure. (Pre-packing also gives you peace of mind and time to clear out the refrigerator.)

- Place cufflinks and studs in plastic or felt containers and put them in one of your jacket pockets.

- If you're traveling with more than one suitcase, number your suitcases and catalog items by suitcase as you pack.

Packing your garment bag

There are many different types and sizes of garment bags on the market. Some of them have built-in frames, and others simply are heavy material designed to cover your clothes. Depending on the specific type of garment bag you have, the following suggestions will assist you in packing it more successfully.

- When packing a garment bag, use a maximum of three hangers. Begin by placing the bag on a flat surface. Layer your clothes as follows. Place pants on a flat surface and fold the top pant leg back in half. Slip hanger on bottom pant leg to knee. Fold bottom pant leg to crotch over the hanger. Fold top pant leg over the hanger and the other pant leg. This method secures the pants to the hanger without having to use clothespins or safety pins.

- Next, place shirts (buttoning them up as you go) over the pants and jackets. Cover each hanger with dry-cleaner bags once all the clothes have been hung on them.

- Place dresses on the next hanger and cover them with dry-cleaner bags, which help protect them and keep wrinkles to a minimum.

- After you have all your clothes on the hangers, place your robe or overcoat around all of the clothing. Place this bundle inside your garment bag.

- Gently fold up any garments at the bottom if they are longer than the garment bag. (If one is provided, secure the strap of the garment bag around the center of the bundle.)

- Place rolled knit items where you folded your long items to avoid wrinkles.

- Stuff any additional packing space around the hangers either with socks and shoes or rolled-up knit clothes. Be sure to pad high-heeled shoes or any sharp items so as not to damage your clothing or your bag.

- The biggest mistake most people make when they pack garment bags is not packing enough into them to keep items from shifting. This oversight often results in everything falling to the bottom of the bag. On the other hand, don't overpack your garment bag or it will be cumbersome to carry.

Additional hints for packing a garment bag

- Use wide rubber bands or twist-ties to band hangers together and keep them from falling and snagging clothes.

- Place garments that wrinkle easily at the back of the bag (closest to the outside). There will be less pressure on them and they'll be less likely to wrinkle. .

- Don't forget luggage straps that mainly are used around the girth of hard luggage. Luggage straps are a terrific way to keep your garment bag together, especially when you're carrying it. Be sure to secure the hook inside your bag either by strapping it in the original closing or by using a piece of string or a twist-tie. (A porter once told me that the best way to never see your bag again is if it hooks the fellow who's transferring it.)

- Purchase inexpensive mini-locks to keep zippers closed on the bag's outside pockets.

When you're packing for a vacation

1. Make a complete inventory of what's in your suitcases.
2. Print your name, address and phone number on an index card and place the card in your suitcase before closing. It may prove helpful in identifying your bag if your tags are lost or destroyed.
3. Swap some packed clothing with your traveling partner and use each other's suitcase, just in case one bag is lost or delayed.
4. Take a second pair of eyeglasses. Pack them in a sock and place in your suitcase.

Bill Sutherland
Vice President, Travel
Providence, R.I.

- When checking a garment bag at the airport, be sure to ask at the ticket counter for a bag or cardboard box to help protect it. Some airlines provide these free of charge, and they help keep your bag looking new.

- When carrying a garment bag on the plane, try to make sure it's stowed near you.

- Don't pack valuables in your garment bag in case it's moved out of your sight.

Additional luggage tips

- Compression bags let you roll the air out of bulky clothes, giving you 75 percent more space in the bag.

- Don't buy cheap luggage. You're not buying it for one trip, but — hopefully — many trips.

- Get luggage with wheels and collapsible handles.

- Make sure your rolling luggage has rubber or plastic "skids" to keep bags from getting scuffed when going over curbs.

- Repairable zippers are imperative. If these zippers come off the track or get out of alignment, you can run them back and forth over the trouble spot and they "repair" themselves.

Luggage identification tips

- Most bags look more or less alike. Individualizing your bag is very important. Should it become lost or delayed in transit, it makes it much easier for baggage personnel to track it down by looking for a distinctive marking on your bag. Bear in mind, they see thousands of the same makes and brands of suitcases every week. Here are some ways to make your bag more easily identifiable:

  ✓ Colorful garment straps around the outside of the bag

  ✓ A little pompom attached to the strap or handle

  ✓ A colorful ID tag. Use several on different sides of your bag so it can be identified from any angle.

  ✓ Colorful tape

- Put identification tags on all bags, including tote bags and carry-on bags.

- When preparing luggage identification tags, never put your home address on the tag. Use the address and phone number of a family member or your travel agent, or whoever else has agreed to be your home contact person. In the event that you and your luggage become separated, the contact person will be able to tell the airline where to send your luggage. This technique also keeps thieves from knowing that you're out of town.

Luggage locks

- Luggage locks are important. I recommend using combination locks rather than key locks, so you don't have to hassle with keys or worry about losing them.

- Customs officials sometimes will cut locks off to get in a bag. To prevent this, you can leave your (opened) lock in your bag with a note to customs saying, "Would you mind attaching this lock when you're finished looking through my bag? Thanks."

- Retractable cable locks are great for bag security in a variety of places — train stations, airports, luggage racks in train compartments, etc. With a retractable cable lock you can secure a bunch of bags together, making it difficult for a thief to grab one.

More packing and luggage-related tips

- Start with a checklist of what you intend to take and check items off the list as you pack them. Be sure to pack your checklist and take it with you so you'll remember what you brought and where you packed it (especially helpful on extended trips where you fully unpack at your destination). Keep the checklist for your next trip and make notes of what to revise — that is, things you didn't use or need. This will help you pack lighter on subsequent trips.

- Take a photo of all your luggage and the contents (when it's laid out, before you put it in the bag), including your carry-on bag. That way, if your bag is lost, stolen or delayed, you can provide a photo to make identification and reclamation easier. Polaroid cameras and digital cameras make this tip easy to implement.

- Pack lots of plastic bags (preferably resealable ones) in various sizes to hold jewelry, wet swimsuits, cosmetics and laundry.

- Pack your toiletries one to two days in advance and then go through your normal routine. Check to make sure that everything you need is ready to go. Remember that trial sizes of everything save space. Who needs 12 ounces of shampoo for a one-week trip?

- Do not fill bottles to the top with liquids. Squeeze out excess air and put tape around the top for added protection. This helps prevent spillage caused by pressure on your bag and changing air pressure when flying.

- For security reasons, *never* carry anything for anyone for any reason.

- If you're pressed for space, wear your heaviest clothing instead of packing it.

- Pack your underwear in mesh laundry bags to save space and make clothes easily available for washing.

- Don't forget the old trick of hanging wrinkled items in a bathroom full of steam to help smooth them out.

- Save the inserts of perfume and cologne samples from magazines and your monthly bills to use when traveling. You won't have to worry about bottles breaking.

- When packing for a trip that might include inclement weather or exposure to water (ferries, tour boats, cruise ships, rafting, a day at the beach or the pool, etc.), be sure to pack a one-time-use waterproof camera.

- To save valuable luggage space, pack clothing that layers well. One of my favorite things to pack in this regard is silk long underwear. A long-sleeved top and long bottoms can be worn under your clothing for warmth, and they also make great pajamas. Silk long underwear is light, incredibly space-saving and can be washed out in the sink and hung up to dry overnight.

- Tissues are more valuable than money in some situations. Pack plenty of travel-size packages of tissues throughout your luggage for easy access any time, any place.

- Never travel with or pack expensive jewelry. It's just not worth the worry. If you want to take some jewelry for a dress-up occasion, I suggest rhinestones or faux pearls — all of the dazzle and none of the worry.

- Pack at least one scarf. Scarves can be used to cover your head not only for warmth but when entering temples or mosques where head coverings may be required.

- Call ahead to see if your hotel provides a hairdryer so you can leave yours at home.

Five great accessories to take with you

Converter for portable electronic devices — Electrical outlets are not standardized around the world. Make sure your portable electronic devices will work and won't get damaged before you plug in far from home. A small, portable converter with multiple adaptation options is just the ticket.

Inflatable neck pillow — Absolutely essential for long flights, train trips and many other travel situations. If you have to sleep in a seated or partially reclined posture, an inflatable neck pillow will help keep you from getting a crick in your neck. Required equipment — and easily packable since it deflates to practically nothing.

Eye shades — Another essential item for sleeping in transit or in places where it's hard to block out either daylight or streetlights any other way.

Ear plugs — Ear plugs keep out unwanted noise so you can sleep or concentrate on reading even if a 2-year-old is having a fit a few rows ahead of you.

Wheeled luggage — One of the great triumphs of human civilization. I simply can't recommend wheeled luggage often enough or strongly enough. Do yourself a favor: Get some before you go on your next trip. And donate your good, usable luggage without wheels to your favorite charity.

✔ Carry-on bag

- Anything of real value (besides what's in your money belt)
- Prescription medications
- Your second pair of glasses
- Camera/film
- Address book, contact information
- Travel alarm clock
- Portable music player for CDs or tapes
- Reading material (book, magazine, newspaper, guide-books, maps, etc.)

- Water, healthy snacks
- In-flight toiletries as needed (toothbrush, toothpaste, contact lenses, case, solution, comb and brush, make-up kit, personal hygiene items, etc.)
- Inflatable neck pillow, eye shades, earplugs
- Mini-flashlight
- Lightweight, collapsible tote bag
- Duplicate passport photos
- Travel-size tissues

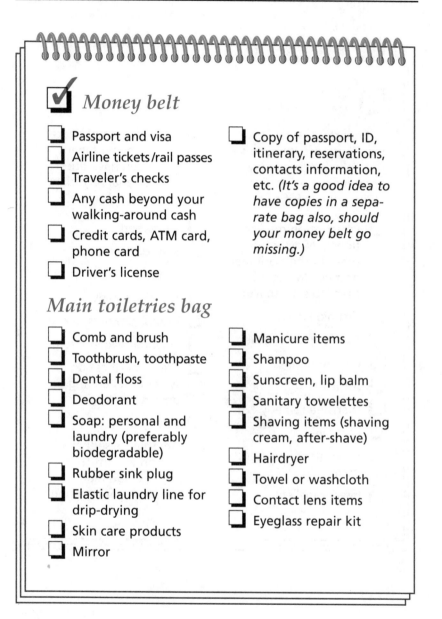

☑ *Money belt*

- ☐ Passport and visa
- ☐ Airline tickets/rail passes
- ☐ Traveler's checks
- ☐ Any cash beyond your walking-around cash
- ☐ Credit cards, ATM card, phone card
- ☐ Driver's license

- ☐ Copy of passport, ID, itinerary, reservations, contacts information, etc. *(It's a good idea to have copies in a separate bag also, should your money belt go missing.)*

Main toiletries bag

- ☐ Comb and brush
- ☐ Toothbrush, toothpaste
- ☐ Dental floss
- ☐ Deodorant
- ☐ Soap: personal and laundry (preferably biodegradable)
- ☐ Rubber sink plug
- ☐ Elastic laundry line for drip-drying
- ☐ Skin care products
- ☐ Mirror

- ☐ Manicure items
- ☐ Shampoo
- ☐ Sunscreen, lip balm
- ☐ Sanitary towelettes
- ☐ Shaving items (shaving cream, after-shave)
- ☐ Hairdryer
- ☐ Towel or washcloth
- ☐ Contact lens items
- ☐ Eyeglass repair kit

☑ *Medications*

Important note: This is a highly personal area of packing. These are items to keep in mind, but by no means the only items you may need to bring. If you have questions, make sure you consult with your personal physician about your specific needs.

- ☐ Prescription medications (always keep these in their original bottles; do *not* mix them to save space)
- ☐ First aid kit
- ☐ Aspirin/pain reliever
- ☐ Cold medicine
- ☐ Antacid
- ☐ Diarrhea remedy
- ☐ Laxative
- ☐ All contact lens-related items
- ☐ Insect repellent
- ☐ Sunscreen
- ☐ Sunburn remedy
- ☐ Antibiotic cream
- ☐ Jet-lag remedy
- ☐ Motion sickness remedy
- ☐ Personal hygiene items
- ☐ Water purification system (depending on destination)
- ☐ Vitamins
- ☐ Anything else that's not on this list that your personal physician tells you to bring

☑ *Maintenance items*

Yes, you'll notice some items from other lists, but this can be a helpful checklist grouping as well:

- ☐ Miniflashlight/batteries
- ☐ Matches or lighter (but not in checked bags, only on your person)
- ☐ Camera batteries
- ☐ Mini-sewing kit
- ☐ Eyeglass repair kit
- ☐ Duct tape (Here's a tip: Wrap some around a pencil.)
- ☐ Extra resealable bags
- ☐ Elastic laundry line and laundry soap
- ☐ Inflatable hangers

And most importantly, wherever you go and whatever else you bring with you or leave behind, always remember to pack the following:

- ☐ Your sense of humor
- ☐ Your respect for people of different cultures

CHAPTER 9

Tips and Tactics for Sane Family Travel

*Cool, calm and
(hopefully) collected
theories of relativity*

A VERY PERSONAL OPINION ABOUT FAMILY TRAVEL

Throughout this book, I've included information I hope will be useful to families. In that sense, this isn't the only family travel chapter, strictly speaking. Even so, the subject of family travel could be its own multivolume book. I believe travel is one of the best educations parents can give their children. It's a catalyst for wonderful memories that last a lifetime and a powerful vehicle for family bonding and communication. Even its mishaps can provide comedy material for years to come. I advocate it unequivocally. Start traveling with your children as soon as you can. Show them the world. Don't wait until you have the time. Don't wait until you have the money. Family travel is one of the few things that's actually worth putting on credit cards if that's the only option you have at the time. And that's not a payment strategy I advocate lightly.

PLAN TOGETHER

As I said in Chapter 1, there are great democratic principles that can be applied to family travel.

Such as?

We hold these truths to be self-evident: When you travel with a group, there has to be something in the trip for everyone or the road gets bumpy fast. Grandma probably doesn't care to Rollerblade through Central Park, but maybe she'd like to get a cup of tea and read her book or spend some time at the Metropolitan Museum of Art while you and the kids race around. (Apologies to the Rollerblading grandmothers of the world.)

The point is, group travel works best when everyone has a say. Make a list. Take an opinion poll. Get kids involved in planning the trip and your activities. Look for mutual interests. Create constructive compromises to avoid unnecessary conflict. It's good family politics.

Don't worry, parents, I'm not suggesting that everyone is in charge just because they get to put their two cents in. Vacation planning is a lot like real democracy: Somebody still has to take *charge*, and just because we want something, that doesn't mean we can afford to pay for it. Whatever your budget is, when you select a travel destination, make sure it can accommodate activities that are as diverse as the people — and the ages of the people — in your group.

Let's talk family values

Communication is the family value. The foundation. The keystone. The starting block. The departure point. The first step. The cat's meow. The bee's knees. The rat's rompers.

What's eating your family travel budget?

Eating out can be a fun part of any family trip, but it's also expensive. Nothing cuts into the family travel budget like feeding the entire crew three restaurant meals a day. A family of four eating at a fast-food place can easily spend $20 or more for lunch. Unless you've specifically budgeted for this expense, consider this cost-cutting alternative: the grocery store.

A well-stocked cooler that can be refilled with ice and groceries along the way literally can save you hundreds, even thousands of dollars in the course of a family vacation. Breakfast and lunch are particularly well-suited to this portable meal plan. The great part is you save money and have more fun.

OK, the kids-under-17-stay-free policy found at some family hotels is a close second. But I'd still put communication as the top link in the family values food chain.

And one of two things can happen to communication on a family trip:

1. It can break down faster than an old car that's 2½ quarts low on oil.

Or...

2. It actually can happen.

I personally believe it's a mistake for parents to feel like it's their job to keep kids entertained every waking minute of a trip. An important part of family travel is kids learning how to keep themselves entertained, learning to appreciate the journey itself rather than thinking of travel time as the boring thing that happens before you get to the amusement park or the hotel with a pool.

Get kids involved in the journey. Teach them to read a map. Show them the sites. Plan stops at historic landmarks, national parks, state parks, museums, scenic vistas. Look at the maps and travel guides before you go. See what's readily accessible along the way. Use your in-transit time as a way to engage kids, to teach and show them new things, to talk with them.

Five safety tips for traveling with children

1. Always carry recent, high-quality photos of each child you're traveling with.
2. Show your kids how to lock hotel room doors, how to call for help on a phone, and make sure they know where the emergency exits are wherever you're staying.
3. If your child is under the age of 1, he should be seated in a rear-facing infant seat and placed in the back seat. If your child is age 1 to 4, he should be in a forward-facing child safety seat in the back seat. A child older than 4 should have an appropriate restraint to help the lap and shoulder belt fit correctly.
4. Don't leave kids alone in the car, even briefly.
5. Make sure older siblings know that they have a responsibility to help you keep an eye on their younger brothers and sisters, and that you expect them to take this responsibility seriously.
6. Teach your child to yell, "This is not my mom or dad," if anyone tries to get the child to leave with them.

For those parents who may be rolling their eyes right now, let me just say: I'm not trying to be overly optimistic or naïve about the difficulties of traveling with children. Everyone needs a little downtime; an occasional movie in the VCR may be relaxing.

Things you want to say as little as possible on your family vacation: the parents' edition

1. "Don't *make* me pull this car over!"
2. "I don't care who started it. Be quiet."
3. "I told you to go to the bathroom before we left the house/restaurant/rest stop/bathroom."

Things you want to say as little as possible on your family vacation: the kids' edition

1. "Mom! Dad! No! Don't pull the car over! We'll stop, we swear!"
2. "He started it!"
3. "But I have to go *now*."

Traveling with your parents or grandparents

Planning ahead and being considerate of unique needs are the two keys to traveling with your parent, grandparent, aunt or uncle. Here are some ways to make the trip go more smoothly:

1. If you're traveling internationally with a parent or grandparent, make sure all paperwork is in order and up-to-date. Are passports and visas current? Assist them in getting traveler's checks and local currencies.

2. Make sure all prescription medicine is up-to-date and sufficient quantities have been packed for the trip.

3. Is insurance up-to-date? Does it include coverage for interstate or international travel? When in doubt, check with the insurance company.

4. Consider food restrictions. You can call airlines ahead and request special meals when you book your trip.

5. Be reasonable about the pace of your day and planned activities. Plan rest breaks, regular bathroom stops and keep walking distances to a length that can be handled without getting too fatigued.

6. Leave extra time. Feeling rushed is stressful for everyone. Leave plenty of time to check in at the airport. Take advantage of pre-boarding calls for flights. Wherever you're going, however you're getting there, leave yourself extra time.

7. Help with packing and luggage requirements. Make sure suitcases have wheels and retractable handles. Be sure you can carry everything if your traveling companions are unable to carry their own luggage.

8. Check with the hotel when reserving accommodations. Do they have elevators? Quiet rooms?

9. Don't assume, ask. Most people are happy to travel with their families and are glad to have your assistance. But be respectful. Ask questions, make suggestions, but don't make assumptions. Check with them.

Bonus round: "Are we there yet?"

Hint: "If you have to ask, the answer is still no."

Yes, there comes that time in every parent's life when you realize you just said something that, up until this moment in your life, you'd only ever heard your mother say.

SPATIAL RELATIONS

There's an inverse relationship between transportation space and trouble. The less personal space everyone has (especially children), the more potential there is for trouble.

Helpful preoccupations

A parent friend of mine once said, only half jokingly I suspect, that parenthood sometimes can feel like an elaborate system of bribes or trying to negotiate with a Third World dictator who hasn't had his nap or a juice box.

Children can be maddeningly difficult to reason with at times, which is why we sometimes bribe them with sugar and TV. But they are fundamentally simple creatures. Like most people, they're a lot more reasonable when they're not:

1. Hungry
2. Tired
3. Too hot
4. Too cold
5. Some combination of the four

Good nutrition (that is, keeping the sugar and junk food intake to a reasonable level) and temperature-control tactics are key in keeping kids happy and parents sane. Here are some additional tips for traveling harmoniously with children:

• Bring along favorite games, toys and books. Pack these in a backpack to keep the car neat and also allow easy access.

• Bring tapes or CDs of music and stories they enjoy that you can play in the car along the way.

• Make sure kids are comfortably dressed for travel. Loose-fitting clothes and comfortable walking shoes are a good place to start. Be sure you can add or subtract layers of clothing to accommodate fluctuating temperatures.

• Bring along treats or rewards like favorite snacks and small gifts.

- Duffel bags are perfect for packing large items like car seats and strollers. Get one with wheels.
- Take regular breaks. Get out of the car, walk around, throw a ball. Exercise and fresh air keep kids (and parents) from getting stir-crazy on long road trips.
- Make sure everyone's used the restroom before getting back in the car.
- Keep as close as possible to their normal routines.
- Count your bags and family members as often as possible. You don't want to misplace either along the way.

VISITING RELATIVES — BE A GOOD GUEST
Good manners keep the peace

OK, this is another one of those potentially touchy subjects. The following tips are offered for your consideration.

Visiting your relatives can be like visiting a foreign country. You want to be sensitive to the native inhabitants and their ways, but without

Get to know your national parks

History and scenery on a budget

The United States national park system stretches from sea to shining sea, Acadia to Zion. From the Badlands in South Dakota to wetlands in Key Biscayne and canyons in Moab, Utah, national parks have something for everyone. Canyons, caves, craters, mountains and molehills. Petrified trees and live ones that are bigger and older than you'd thought possible.

The national parks are a natural treasure, and they're still a bargain — especially for family travel. National parks offer an extraordinary array of recreational activities, lodging and camping options that won't break your budget.

For $50, you can get an annual pass that provides free admission for the whole family at any national park in the country, at a AAA office or at aaa.com. The National Park Service has a great website (ParkNet) at nps.gov, or you can get more information by calling them at 1-888-GoParks (467-2757).

compromising your own identity and independence too much. Be the kind of guest in their home that you would want them to be in yours. Even among the happiest families, there are certain things that can stir up discontent in the course of a visit. Here are some common potential friction points and ways to avoid them. Most adults know this stuff, but be sure your kids do, too. Talk with them before you arrive.

- **The bathroom:** Observe good etiquette. Don't leave towels on the floor, hair in the drain or stubble in the sink. Bring your own toiletries.
- **The kitchen:** Don't leave a mess. Tidy up your own dishes. Put food away. Offer to help or just pitch in without asking or having to be asked to do so (but defer to the host or hostess regarding assistance with cooking or cleaning up). Bring groceries as a gift if you're visiting relatives on a budget and you've got a big family in tow.
- **Other considerations:** Make the bed, or close up the sofa bed when you get up in the morning. Deal with your own laundry: Don't leave it scattered all over the floor. Strip the bed and leave the linens in the room or on the washing machine. Be sensitive about the noise level. Don't let your kids run amok. Defer to the household rules. Make sure your kids know what these rules are.

Sometimes there are logistical difficulties that don't preclude a friendly visit but make staying under the same roof impractical or inadvisable. Don't overlook these things just to save a buck on lodgings Family harmony and your sanity are much more important than saving money on a hotel room. Be realistic and don't assume the house is child-friendly. Check for safety issues and bring a nightlight for the younger kids.

AND LAST, BUT NOT LEAST . . . PETS

Pets: We love them and they love us. But they do have special needs. Whether your pet stays behind or comes with you, proper care is extremely important for pets, so you should start planning for it early on.

Before you go

- Make sure your pet is in good health. All shots should be up-to-date. When in doubt, call your vet and schedule a checkup. If your pet requires prescription medication, make sure you bring enough to last your entire trip. Never assume it will be easy to refill a prescription on the road.

- Be sure your pet's collar is in good, sturdy condition and that the tag is up to date. Attach an ID tag with your contact information to the pet's collar. Consider making a temporary tag with contact information for your destination.

- If your pet can't actively participate in the trip, maybe your friend should stay home.

- If your pet is subject to car sickness, don't feed it for 12 hours before departure time.

- If you'll be staying in hotels along the way, call ahead. Make reservations at pet-friendly accommodations ahead of time. Don't assume a hotel accepts pets. Always check first.

- If you're taking your pet with you on a car trip, be sure you know how your pet responds to traveling in the car before you go. Most dogs love being in the car; cats generally are less enthused. Know before you go.

- Pack everything your pet will need for the trip: food, water, bowls, toys, leash, medications (as needed), cleanup kit, sleeping pad and portable kennel. Put food in tough, resealable plastic containers so it doesn't make a mess. Have a separate crate or bag for all pet items so they don't get lost or misplaced inside the vehicle.

- If you're crossing borders, know the rules for pets before you go. An easy way to do this is to either check with your vet or a travel agent about specific rules for different countries.

- If your pet is traveling by plane, be sure to book its transport when scheduling your own.

Pets in transit

- If your pet suffers from anxiety when being transported in the car or by plane, talk to your vet. There are mild sedatives for cats and dogs that can relieve their anxiety and help them sleep.

- Always bring a cleanup kit with you should your pet get sick in the car or have an unfortunate accident. Paper towels, plastic baggies and spray disinfectant/cleaner can really come in handy.

- Keep your pet on the leash. It's important to give your pet regular rest stops for food, water, exercise and bathroom breaks, but it's bad news if pets run loose in an unfamiliar area or anywhere near the freeway.

Additional tips for traveling with children

Most safety tips about traveling with children boil down to one simple rule: Keep an eye on them. Children don't necessarily need to know how much we worry about them, but they do need to know the rules for safety and take these rules seriously. Here are some tips for the whole family:

1. Keep track of each other and stay together. Whether you're in an airport, at an amusement park or at a sight-seeing destination, make sure your kids know where to go should they become lost or separated from you. Let them know who to talk to (police, uniformed airport personnel, park rangers, for example). Let them know about paging systems at airports and train stations, and whenever possible make sure you give them a map of where you are. Pick a meeting place for everyone to go to as quickly as possible if you become separated. Buy and use walkie talkies if possible.

2. Whenever you move on, whether you're leaving the hotel, the rest stop, wherever, take a head count. Make sure everyone's present and accounted for.

3. Don't leave kids alone. Go with them to public restrooms, snack bars or video-games area.

4. Make sure you have a family plan for what to do if you become separated. Some families issue whistles for certain situations (hiking and camping trips, for example). Make sure your children have complete contact information on their person (their name, each parent's or guardian's name, home address and phone number, parent or guardian's cell phone number, hotel address and phone number).

5. Make sure children understand that they're not to talk to strangers or accept gifts from people they don't know. Teach your kids to raise a ruckus if someone they don't know tries to physically coerce them in any way.

- Ideally, your pet should know and respond to basic commands. This makes traveling with dogs (because, let's face it, cats won't do anything you tell them) a much safer and more pleasant experience for all concerned.

- Wherever you go, clean up after your pet (meaning, bring lots of bags).

- If you're leaving your pet in the hotel room while you're out, you either should crate it or at least leave the "Do Not Disturb" sign on the door so that you don't give the housekeeper a heart attack.

- Don't leave your pet alone if it's a constant barker. Always be considerate of others and keep your pet quiet.

- Cats always should be transported in a cat carrier on car trips rather than allowing them to roam about the car. Many cats have been lost at rest stops, never to be seen again after making a quick getaway from the car.

- Always bring a carrier for your cat and a tether for your dog when traveling by car. Should you break down and have to leave your car, you'll want to be able to take your pet with you.

CHAPTER 10

SECURING THE HOME FRONT

*Tips and tactics for
leaving everything in order
at home*

GETTING YOUR LIFE (AND YOUR PEACE OF MIND) IN ORDER BEFORE YOU GO

So you're all set to head out on your big vacation. Wonderful. No problem.

Are you sure? Maybe you forgot something important.

Yikes.

Niggling questions and troubling little doubts do not make good traveling companions. Let's say you're 200 miles from home cruising happily down the highway, music playing, windows rolled down to catch the breeze, children getting along, sun shining, birds singing, when your spouse suddenly turns to you with a worried look and says, "Um...honey? Are you sure you remembered to turn the burner off after serving up the oatmeal this morning?"

There are two possible answers to this question:

1. "Yes, honey, I'm absolutely certain. No need to worry."

2. "Hmm. Well...I...you know...I think so, but I'm not absolutely certain."

The second answer is *always* the wrong answer. Many travelers have unhappily but quickly turned around because of it. Be sure you're not among these backtrackers. Be sure you've thought of everything and can give answer No. 1 with total confidence.

PEACE-OF-MIND CHECKLISTS

The home edition

What do you need to do to protect your home while you're off traveling? Most of us think in terms of burglary prevention. That's important, but there's more to it than that. Home preparation falls into three basic categories that I call...

SECURITY, SANITATION, SAVINGS
Security checklist

- Stop deliveries, especially the newspaper.
- Have the post office hold your mail.
- Set up a timed lighting system.
- Turn on your alarm system.
- Notify the local police of your absence.
- Turn down phone ringers or set your voicemail/message machine to pick up after one or two rings.
- Store valuables (jewelry, important files, family heirlooms) in a safe place.
- Eliminate possible fire hazards (unplug appliances, make sure nothing blocks heat ducts or is too close to baseboard heaters).
- Lock all doors and windows. Deadbolt doors and make sure sliding glass doors and windows have slide locks and holding bars in place.
- Ensure your homeowner's insurance is up-to-date.

Sanitation checklist

- Arrange for care of pets, lawn and houseplants as needed.
- Empty your refrigerator (and other food storage areas) of perishable foods.
- Take out the trash. (I know this one seems obvious, but it's amazing how often trash underneath the sink gets forgotten.)
- If you leave trash out for pickup, have a neighbor put the cans back in their proper place.
- Do the dishes.
- Change the kitty litter. Whether the cat's staying or going with you, this is a good way to minimize odor in a closed-up house.

Savings (money, electricity, wear and tear)

- Make sure your bills are paid ahead so you don't accrue late fees or extra interest while you're gone.
- Turn off the water heater. This is optional, of course, but if you're going to be gone a long time, this can save you money on your electric bill.

- Check to make sure faucets inside and outside the house are turned off and not dripping. (Most people don't leave the water running, but you always feel better if you know you checked all the faucets before you left.)

- Turn down the thermostat — but not all the way down if it's February and 27 degrees outside. About 62 degrees or so should suffice to keep the plants alive and the electric bill reined in.

- Turn off home computers and then check them; sometimes screensavers can make them look off when they're not.

BONUS ROUND —SAFETY

- Are you sure you remembered to turn off the burner?

Home contact person checklist

Whenever possible, you should arrange to have one or more home-contact individual who can be your support system on the home front. A trusted friend, relative or neighbor — someone you can get a hold of easily if you need to. Maybe you have one person to take care of household things and another person who keeps important information handy. However you divide the tasks (and if you're lucky, one person can do it all for you), here are some things you may need a home contact person for:

- Pet sitting
- House sitting
- Watering yard and houseplants
- Mail and paper pickup if you don't want to have them held
- Someone to leave a spare house key and/or car key with in case of emergency
- Someone who can reset your house and/or car alarm should they go off

Mandatory go-to person at home

Most importantly — and I think this is essential, not optional — you should have a trusted home contact person who has all your information handy: itinerary, contact numbers where you're staying, reservation/confirmation numbers for your transportation and lodging, a copy of your passport information, toll-free numbers for your credit card companies, traveler's check numbers, contact information for family members or friends in case of emergency, doctor's number, copies of prescription information.

You'll probably never have to make use of this person. But making sure there's someone at home who's got all your important trip information in a file folder can save you a lot of trouble should you find yourself in a jam a long way from home. This may be the single most important tip I can give you about preparing the home front before you go.

FINAL THOUGHTS ABOUT ASSURING YOURSELF A HAPPY HOMECOMING

Leave it the way you want to come back to it

I strongly recommend leaving your home in the condition you'd like to find it when you return. This notion often gets ignored or de-prioritized in the last-minute packing frenzy and to-do listing that is so often the pre-departure experience.

It's human nature to look forward to a vacation, but even though we don't want to think about it when we're beachcombing in Maui, the return day always comes. Plan wisely for it. Don't make it any more difficult or demoralizing than it has to be. Travelers often experience some degree of post-vacation letdown when returning from a trip.

There are ways to minimize that. In addition to the checklists of essential pre-departure considerations, I recommend leaving yourself enough time to do a really bang-up job of housecleaning before you go. I know this does not sound fun, but you will love yourself for it when you return home, and it will make your life much easier.

Obviously, it doesn't take a rocket scientist or a Zen master to know that leaving a sink full of dirty dishes or a pail full of garbage in the kitchen will guarantee an unpleasant, unsanitary and odiferous homecoming from a two-week vacation. Anybody who hasn't figured that one out yet has an object lesson ripening for them in the future.

Most of us have enough presence of mind to remember that the garbage and the dishes need to be taken care of before we leave home. But I also suggest leaving yourself ample time to clean the bathrooms, tidy up the house, deal with any perishable food inside (and outside) of the fridge, vacuum/dust, get your desk organized, put any backlog of mail and paperwork in order and change the kitty litter.

Yes, I know this is not my most popular travel tip, but I stand by it because it's a good one.

It's all about making your homecoming experience as smooth a landing as possible. Remember, when you get back from your trip, you'll have to deal with unpacking, doing laundry, restocking the grocery supplies, catching up on your e-mail, your snail mail and — if you're jet-lagged or coming from another time zone — your sleep. Smart travelers don't just plan well for the departure, they give thoughtful consideration to the return. It may be the last stage of the journey, but don't ignore its importance.

And while we're on the subject of happy returns and how to have them ...

Cushy landings begin with a buffer zone day

Even the most experienced travelers sometimes neglect to give themselves what you might call a "buffer zone day" when returning to their day-to-day home lives. Don't burn out on your re-entry into the home atmosphere. If you get back from an overseas flight on Sunday night at 9 p.m. and have to be at work by 8 a.m. Monday, you're setting yourself up for a lot of unnecessary stress and exhaustion.

Why help the world undo all the good your vacation did you? You'll be stressed out again soon enough when you see what's waiting for you on your desk. Everyone wants to stretch their vacation out as long as possible. But giving yourself a day back to unpack, unwind and catch up is a much better way to it.

As the adage goes, a journey is a circle, and you come back to where you started.

Make sure the kitty litter's fresh when you do.

CHAPTER 11

LAST-MINUTE DETAILS
THAT MATTER

*Or "What do you mean
you're 'pretty sure'
you didn't leave the oven on?!"*

THE BEST TIP ABOUT LAST-MINUTE DETAILS

Try to have as few of them as possible. When you're looking forward to your vacation, time moves about as fast as an elephant in the deep end of a swimming pool full of cold oatmeal. Then, miraculously, a week or so before your scheduled departure, time suddenly compresses down to nothing, picks up speed and becomes a hummingbird on an espresso binge. Pre-departure to-do lists go from being advisory to compulsory, palms get sweaty, pulse rates rise, tempers shorten, and things get forgotten.

Don't let this happen to you.

The *Random House Dictionary* describes *foresight* as "care in planning and preparing for the future." It's kind of an old-fashioned word and idea, I suppose, but it's one of the modern traveler's greatest assets. Foresight: Don't leave home without it.

But *do* leave yourself time before you go — time to plan, time to prepare, time to put your mind at rest, knowing that you really did think of everything. Look over your checklists from previous chapters. Have you packed what you need? Do you have all the important documents and methods of payment you'll need? Is your house in order? Everything you think of before you go is one less thing you'll have to worry about once you've gone.

Here are some last-minute details that may matter to you.

If you're flying

- Confirm your ride to the airport with the person who's driving you. Leave plenty of time. Confirm your ride with the shuttle service if necessary. If you're taking a cab, call well in advance — especially during peak travel times. City dwellers: Is your flight scheduled near morning or evening rush hour? If so, remember to factor in extra transportation time to the airport.

- Confirm your flight at least 48 hours before your scheduled departure. Confirm it again on the day of your departure. Lots of people do this using airlines' toll-free numbers, which is fine, but it's extremely easy (and often faster) to confirm flight information on a carrier's website.

- Given security precautions and possible delays associated with them, arrive at the airport at least two hours prior to your departure for domestic flights, three to four hours before your departure on an international flight. If you have any questions about security delays, how crowded the airport is or if there are traffic delays around the airport, call your carrier's toll-free number, airport information or your travel agent.

- Before you go, make absolutely sure you've got your ticket and itinerary with you. If you're using an e-ticket, you must have either a receipt for your e-ticket (including the ticket number) OR an itinerary generated by a travel agency or airline confirming an electronic ticket (including the ticket number).

- Reconfirm any special meals that you may have requested at booking.

If you're driving

- Have your car serviced by a reputable auto technician or a AAA Approved Auto Repair facility.

- Fill up the gas tank well before your scheduled departure time.

- Change your oil shortly before you depart. Always check your engine oil level right before you leave, regardless. Sometimes it can "settle" half a quart after an oil change. Bring at least one extra quart with you for the road.

The glove compartment top 10 list

 Does anybody actually put gloves in the glove compartment anymore? If so, forgive me for leaving them off the top 10 list. Too often the glove compartment gets treated as an auxiliary trash dumpster, when it really needs to be a mini-support system center for the driver. Before you go, clean it out, get it organized and have some essentials handy. For more info, see Chapter 13, Car Travel.

1. Crucial paperwork: proof of insurance, vehicle registration, owner's manual for the vehicle, repair manual or repair records
2. Cell phone
3. Flashlight with extra batteries
4. Tire pressure gauge
5. Small first aid kit
6. Pen and paper
7. Maps and/or pocket road atlas
8. Spare pair of sunglasses
9. Travel-size pack of tissues and moist sanitary wipes
10. Pocket knife or all-in-one tool

- Check all other fluid levels: windshield washer fluid, radiator coolant, brake fluid and transmission fluid. If you don't know how to do this, have your mechanic check fluid levels.

- Check headlights, brakelights and turn signals to ensure you're safe *and* legal.

- Replace windshield wiper blades as needed. If they're worn but hanging in there, replace them anyway or bring some spares with you. Road trips can be hard on windshield wipers, and they're an important safety consideration. You don't want to have to worry about

Before you go, get ready, get set ...

1. Review all travel documents carefully to check their accuracy.
2. Make two copies of your passport, visa, air tickets and other pertinent travel documents. Carry one copy with you — not with the originals — and leave one at home with a relative or friend just in case.
3. Make arrangements for a friend or relative to collect your mail and papers or have your mail and papers held for later delivery. A collection of ungathered mail and newspapers at your house is an invitation for trouble.
4. Make a copy of your itinerary and contact numbers to leave with friends or family.
5. Make sure to take a good supply of film and batteries for your camera. These items can be expensive overseas.
6. Make sure you have an adequate supply of prescription medication and an extra pair of eyeglasses or contact lenses. Stow these in your carry-on.
7. Get traveler's checks for your trip. Do not carry a large amount of cash.
8. Reconfirm your flight 48 hours prior to departure.
9. Arrive at the airport in time: two hours before a domestic flight and three hours before an international flight.

Susan Ledford
AAA General Manager
Hendersonville Service Office, N.C.

replacing them in a rainstorm in the middle of the night in the middle of nowhere.

- Check tires for wear and tear. Don't gamble with your life. If they're worn, balding or damaged, replace them. And don't forget to check the spare tire, too. If it's damaged or deflated, it won't do you any good should you need it. You also should check to make sure your jack is in good working order and that you have a lug wrench/tire iron. I also recommend having a can or two of flat fixer. Even if you have a good spare tire, a tire iron and a working jack, it's good to have a backup plan should you get a flat someplace where you wouldn't want to have to change one.

- Check to be certain child safety seats are in good working condition and properly fastened in place.

- Always carry a sturdy, water-resistant flashlight — and put fresh batteries in it before you go. Bring jumper cables.

- Make sure your auto insurance coverage, driver's license and license plate tags are current. Plan your route in advance; check the map.

- Bring a roll of quarters for tolls and parking meters.

THE DOUBLECHECK CHECKLIST OF CRUCIAL PRE-DEPARTURE ITEMS

Sure, some of these items are trip-specific, and you may not need everything on the list. But before you go, ask yourself, "Do I have my ...?"

- Personal identification such as driver's license, Social Security card, birth certificate, international driving permit

- Passport and/or visa

- Health documentation, prescription-related information and prescription medication

- Transportation tickets

- Itinerary

- Emergency information, home contacts information, travel agent contact information

- Hotel reservations (on paper, if possible)

- Traveler's checks

- Small amount of your destination's local currency ($75-$100 U.S. equivalent)

Resources to keep you in the know before you go

Travel conditions

Good travel agents keep abreast of changing conditions: weather, politics or airline information that could affect your trip and road conditions. When in doubt, check in with your travel agent before you go. Here are some additional online resources to help you stay informed.

Political conditions

The U.S. State Department's website — travel.state.gov — has a wealth of information for travelers, including the latest travel updates and traveler safety reports from the Bureau of Consular Affairs. It also has lists of lawyers and legal resources for travelers abroad, links to foreign embassies, passport and visa information, and foreign entry requirements. These are your tax dollars at work. You paid for this resource, so don't be shy about using it.

Road and weather conditions

A terrific government resource you should take advantage of and not overlook is your state's Department of Transportation website. There are different URLs for each state, so just type in either "Department of Transportation" (and look for individual listings for any states you might be traveling through) or do a keyword search using your state's name and "Department of Transportation." The Department of Transportation has traffic and travel conditions for all 50 states and tons of other information for travelers, including ferry schedules, train schedules and lists of available maps.

Another great resource is AAA. Search the aaa.com website and you'll automatically be routed to your state's AAA site. AAA sites also provide travel and traffic news and safety information, and road and weather conditions.

For the latest traffic and weather updates anywhere in the United States, including current "real-time" information about road closures and construction, check out accutraffic.com.

- Credit cards (two, preferably)
- ATM card
- Phone card
- Trip cancellation insurance, medical insurance documents and policies
- Extra passport photos
- Only the keys needed upon return home (house keys, car keys)
- Photocopies of important documents (passport, visa, tickets, reservations, home contacts/phone number list)
- Toll-free numbers for credit card companies

Protect yourself, protect your vacation

Here's something to consider before you go on your vacation: Travel insurance can protect you and your vacation investment in all sorts of situations, including coverage for emergency medical and dental care, baggage protection, baggage delay (to pay for essential-item purchases if your personal baggage is delayed or misdirected for at least 24 hours), trip cancellation or interruption protection. Contact your travel agent for more information.

THERE'S NO PLACE LIKE HOME

Let's keep it that way

We've covered essential considerations for securing the homefront in the last chapter, but here are some last-minute tips for the road:

- Don't advertise your departure to the world. If possible, pack the car in the garage.

- Provide your house sitter with a complete list of responsibilities, along with detailed, clearly written instructions for pet care, plant care, yard care, alarms and any other relevant item in their care. Don't assume. When in doubt, *overexplain.*

- Be sure you've made your rent or mortgage payment before you go. People sometimes forget to do this when their departure date comes before rent or mortgage payment is due.

- Be sure your renter's or homeowner's insurance is paid up and current.

And, last but not least, do yourself a favor: Make sure all the burners on the stove are off.

Bon voyage!

CHAPTER 12

AIR TRAVEL

*The ups and downs,
ins and outs
of flying*

When I began writing this book, the biggest concern about carry-on baggage was if it fit in the overhead bin or under the seat in front of you.

Things have changed.

As a result, additional restrictions and delays have been imposed on air travel. Personally, I'm glad. I don't think any of us are too busy to donate an hour or two of our time to better security. Airport security is a fluid situation, so the following is where things stand right now. Always seek out the latest information from your specific carrier (call them or surf their website) or from the Federal Aviation Administration (faa.gov) before you fly.

Check-in procedures and bag checks

If it has been awhile since you've flown, the first thing you need to know is to allow yourself more time. Every aspect of airport life — parking, check-in, security checkpoints and boarding — takes longer than it used to.

Passengers are advised to arrive at the airport at least two hours before domestic flights and three hours before international flights. This is the recommendation for "normal" conditions. If you're traveling during peak times, you should consider showing up even earlier. It's also a good idea to check with airport information the day of your departure to find out if things are moving smoothly or are backed up.

For you early birds, remember: Most airlines won't check bags until you're at least within four hours of your flight's departure time.

Check-in procedures are more rigorously enforced. You'll be asked if you packed your own bag and if it has been out of your sight since you packed it. You'll also be asked to show a photo ID (your driver's license) for domestic flights and your passport for international flights. Without proper ID, you'll be denied boarding. Curbside check-in is resuming, but with greater attention to security. Size and weight restrictions for checked bags remain the same. Typically that means a maximum of two checked bags per passenger, not to exceed 70 pounds per bag with a combined height, length and width of 62 inches per bag.

Tip: If you doubt that your bags are compliant with weight and dimension requirements, find out *before* you get to the airport. All you need is a tape measure and a bathroom scale. If your bag is too bulky to fit on the scale, get on the scale while holding your bag, read the weight, set the bag aside and read the scale again. The difference will be your bag's weight. Of course, if your bag is heavy, don't hurt yourself. It's cheaper to pay for the extra weight than hernia surgery.

Carry-on bags

In general, the current standard is one carry-on bag, not to exceed 45 linear inches (9 by 14 by 22 inches), that will fit under the seat or in the overhead bin and one "personal item" — meaning a purse, a brief-case or a laptop. Most airlines count backpacks as carry-on bags, not personal items, so if you have a backpack and a carry-on bag you may have to check one of them. Check with your travel agent and plan accordingly.

The most important new policy you need to know about carry-on bags concerns the contents. Pretty much any sharp object that could be used as a weapon no longer can be brought in carry-on luggage

Tips for personal security and safety

1. Never leave your bags unattended.
2. Don't hang your purse or bag on the hook in the bathroom stall. This gives thieves a snatch-and-run opportunity. (For more tips on luggage security, see Chapter 8.)
3. Be especially careful at security checkpoint conveyor belts and metal detectors. Watch your bag as it goes through the scanning equipment. Don't walk through the metal detector until you can see that your bag is being scanned. There have been incidents when people moving through security checkpoints didn't watch their bag and it was stolen. Don't allow yourself to be distracted. If you're pulled aside for additional scanning, ask to move your bag off the conveyor, or keep it in sight.
4. Be extremely cautious of anyone who tries to get your attention or has a "mishap" that involves you. If someone spills something on you, bumps into you suddenly or otherwise tries to distract you (especially when you're occupied with something else), be suspicious. Keep an eye on them and a hand on your bag. Many scams operate on a variation of what I call the *distraction-then-subtraction* principle (or *lack* of principles as the case may be). In other words, if you get distracted, they get your bag, wallet, camera or whatever.
5. Never carry a package for anyone.

Your favorite little penknife you always keep in your purse or on a key-chain? Forget it. Put it in your checked baggage or leave it at home. If you have any doubts about a particular item, call the airline ahead of time or ask airline personnel at the terminal check-in counter.

Only ticketed passengers are allowed past security checkpoints. So if you have friends or family coming to meet your flight, they'll have to meet you in the baggage claim area or on the other side of the security checkpoint. To get to the gate, you have to prove you've been ticketed for a flight.

So what does this mean for e-ticket passengers?

If you're an e-ticket passenger, you must have either a receipt for your e-ticket (including the ticket number) OR an itinerary generated by a travel agency or airline confirming an electronic ticket (including the ticket number). You may be asked for your ID again as well. Your best bet for passing through security as quickly as possible is to have your receipt, itinerary *and* your photo ID all ready to show as needed.

Final thoughts on security precautions

We live in an open society, and it's difficult to eliminate all elements of risk without eliminating most of the things that make our society worth living in. Obviously, there's room for improvement when it comes to security. But as much as we might want things to change overnight, overhauling airport security procedures is going to take time, patience, persistence and lots of money.

Stay tuned, be safe and Godspeed.

TICKETING TERMS AND TIPS

The pros and cons of getting bumped

Airlines overbook flights, knowing that many people will cancel their reservations or not show up. It's a gamble carriers have to take to keep the planes as full as possible and to minimize revenue loss. Sometimes this overbooking results in too many passengers and not enough seats. That's when passengers get "bumped." This is most like-ly to occur during peak travel times, especially between Thanksgiving and New Year's.

To avoid being bumped, I recommend requesting pre-assigned seating if the airline allows it. Remember to check in for your flight at least 20 minutes prior to departure, or the airline may give your seat away (they have the right to do that).

If it does happen to you, you're entitled to what's known as "denied boarding compensation." Here are the terms:

- If the airline can get you on another flight that will get you to your destination within an hour of your original flight, they are not required to compensate you.

- If your arrival is delayed more than an hour because you got bumped, the airline is required to compensate you the price of your ticket for that leg of the trip (in addition to getting you on another flight), in other words, the price of a one-way ticket.

- If your arrival is delayed more than two hours, you usually are compensated twice the price of your ticket for that leg of the trip (your full round-trip ticket price in most cases).

- Certain conditions and limitations apply. To be eligible for compensation, you have to have confirmed and reconfirmed your ticket. And you must have checked in within the deadline established by the airline. Check your carrier's terms. Generally speaking, late arrivers are the first to be bumped and the last to receive compensation.

Even with compensation, getting bumped can be very inconvenient if you're in a hurry. If you want to minimize your chances of getting bumped, show up in plenty of time, check in and board the plane as soon as you can. If you're already in your seat, they can't bump you, but you can volunteer to be bumped. And why would you *want* to volunteer to be bumped? Because it can work to your advantage if you're on a flexible schedule.

Airlines are required to ask for volunteers before turning away ticketed passengers. It's better public relations to offer passengers cash or lots of free miles to give up their seats than it is to turn people away at the gate. When a flight is overbooked, airline personnel usually will get on the intercom and ask for volunteers who are willing to give up their seats for a free ticket. Watch to see who goes for it. If nobody does, they'll almost always up the ante by offering more miles. By the time they're asking for volunteers inside the cabin of the plane, the deal usually is even sweeter. The trick is in knowing when to jump at the opportunity. Once they've found enough volunteers, the offer is up.

Getting bumped *can* be a good deal, but gauge the value of the compensation versus the time it will take to get where you're going and the possible expense of meals and lodging if you have to wait until the next day for a flight. Whether you receive compensation in the form of a check, tickets or both, you're entitled to have them issued to you right away. Make sure you understand all terms, conditions and restrictions on your re-issued ticket.

To 'e' or not to 'e' (ticket), that is the question

E-tickets have been touted by the airline industry as a great advantage and convenience for travelers. Is this true? Not exactly. "Ticketless travel" saves the airlines a lot of money in printing and paper costs, but it's not always such a wonderful system for passengers. True, you can't lose an e-ticket the way you can a paper ticket. On the other hand, if the airline goes on strike, if your flight is canceled or if the airline's computers go down, you can have a difficult — even impossible — time converting your e-ticket into a ticket to ride. Why is that?

More tips for personal security and safety

1. Do *not* joke around with ticket counter personnel when they ask you if you packed your own bag, if it has been out of your sight or if anyone asked you to carry anything for them. Believe me, they won't think it's funny. They'll take it seriously, and you'll have to take another plane.

2. If you've checked bags, go immediately to the baggage claim area once you've gotten off the plane. Bags are particularly vulnerable to theft on baggage carousels, so get them off the merry-go-round as soon as you can.

3. Stay oriented. Knowing where you are and where you're going is not only less frustrating, it's a good security tip. If you're in an unfamiliar airport, follow signs, look for information desks, ask counter personnel to help you if you get lost. Before your flight even lands, ask a flight attendant to give you directions to your connecting flight's gate, baggage claim, airport information, ground transportation area. They'll be glad to help you.

4. Have an airport map. Here's a great, low-budget way to do this: Most complimentary in-flight magazines — the ones you find in the seat pocket in front of you on the plane — have very handy maps of various airports (generally found toward the back of the magazine). Take the magazine with you and rip out the page or pages with the airport maps you need.

5. Keep valuable documents, tickets, your passport and methods of payment in your security wallet. Security wallets aren't just for international travelers; they come in very handy for domestic travelers who spend time in airports, too.

Because e-tickets are only verifiable online. If a particular airline is having operational difficulties, other airlines often will honor their competitors' tickets in an attempt to win new customers. If you have a paper ticket, you can take advantage of this policy. If you have an e-ticket, the process is more complicated. Because one airline can't access another airline's computer records to verify your e-ticket, it can't be transferred from one airline to another until you first convert it into a paper ticket. And getting your e-ticket converted into a paper ticket when you're in the airport can be a very time-consuming process, requiring you to go back to your airline's terminal check-in counter, stand in line with the other e-ticket holders from your flight and start from the top.

When deciding on whether or not to go the e-ticket route, you also should consider your destination. Since airline computer systems (though imperfect) generally are pretty reliable in the United States, international travelers are more likely to encounter the types of computer problems that make ticketless travel less practical.

Tip: When in doubt, get your ticket printed out.

You can state your preference for paper tickets when you make your reservation with the airline or your travel agent. The airline may charge a $10 to $20 fee for paper tickets, but it can be worth it. Think of the paper ticket fee as the price of peace-of-mind insurance.

Are there any drawbacks to paper tickets? A few. Paper tickets essentially are like cash. If you lose them, it can be a real hassle. Airlines don't have to refund a lost or stolen ticket until it expires unused. In the meantime, you may have to pay in full to get a replacement ticket.

Even so, delays and cancellations simply are less of a hassle if you have a paper ticket.

What about cancellations?

Flight cancellations fall into two categories: those that are the airline's fault and those that aren't. If your flight is delayed or canceled because of weather conditions, your carrier will try to get you on the next possible flight. But airlines are not obligated to provide meals or lodging if bad weather, a natural disaster or other acts of God force flight delays or cancellations.

Delays that are the carrier's fault — such as mechanical problems and scheduling mishaps — obligate the carrier to compensate passengers. Compensation may include lodging, meal vouchers, transportation on alternate carriers and sometimes even phone cards. But if your flight is canceled or the airline was responsible for you missing your flight, you should be able to receive a refund or be rescheduled without any change fees being applied. Some airlines are more gracious than others when it comes to compensation. But savvy air travelers have an ace up their sleeve. It's called "Rule 240."

What is Rule 240?

Rule 240 is something the airlines would rather you didn't know about and, indeed, most air passengers *don't* know about it. The airlines certainly won't bring it up if you don't. But here's the gist: If there's no way that the airline can get you to your destination within two hours of the scheduled arrival time, they have to honor your ticket and get you out on the next scheduled flight — even if it's on *another* airline. Of course, the other airline must have empty seats.

There are a few important "ifs" here. That's *if* the delay is absolutely the airline's fault, *if* it's more than a two-hour delay and *if* you invoke Rule 240. How do you invoke Rule 240? Easy: Go to the counter, present your ticket and say, "I'd like to invoke Rule 240, please" or, "I need you to 240 me, please." They'll know what you mean. And if you've invoked it legitimately, they have no choice and have to honor it.

But I reiterate, 240 doesn't apply to delays — like weather delays — that are in any way not the fault of the carrier. And, you guessed it, you're in a much better position to take advantage of Rule 240 if you're packing a paper ticket instead of an e-ticket.

General ticket tips

- When you get your ticket and itinerary from a travel agent or the airline, check that all the dates, times, connections and fees are correct.

- Airlines can raise ticket prices without notice, which is why you want to book as early as possible and purchase your ticket in advance. You can't be charged extra if you've already purchased your ticket and they raise the price. However, ticket prices also go down, and you're entitled to a refund if you've purchased your ticket for a higher price. The airline will give you the refund, after deducting a $100 fee, and will put the whole amount into a travel voucher for future travel.

- Pay with a credit card — especially a card that gets frequent flyer miles or offers additional coverage. Check with the company or ask your travel agent. Credit card purchases offer protections that you don't get with cash. With credit cards, you can contest charges for goods not received. So if, for example, you were unfortunate enough to purchase a ticket from a shady ticket seller who charges you but never sends the ticket, you're not completely out of luck.

PRE-FLIGHT CONSIDERATIONS
Pre-boarding

Pre-boarding can be a godsend for seniors, parents with infants, passengers with disabilities and anyone who may need a little extra time or assistance getting on the plane. If you have legitimate reasons for pre-boarding, you never should be shy about exercising your right to do so. Airlines also offer members of their frequent-flyer programs a chance to pre-board. It's one of the nice perks of these programs.

Boarding

If your reservation is confirmed and you have your boarding pass in hand, you may want to consider *not* boarding until it's absolutely necessary — especially for long flights. Being on the plane can be fatiguing, so the less time you can spend on it the better. Of course, this strategy can be pushed too far, but that's called "missing your flight."

Overhead bin tip

If you have a carry-on bag that needs to go in the overhead bin, start counting rows and scoping out bin space as soon as you get on the plane. **Tip:** It's better to stow your luggage in an overhead bin in *front* of your seat than behind it. Why? Because you can keep an eye on it in-flight. It also makes boarding and deplaning much easier because you don't have to backtrack up and down the aisle through a crowd to get your bag.

In-flight comforts and considerations

Who *really* likes being on a plane? I do. I enjoy the quiet. There are no phones ringing, no distractions, and I can catch up on reading. I like getting to my destination quickly. I like the view out the window, the land below, the clouds as seen from above or at eye level.

But I'm not crazy about the lack of leg room or trying to eat an airplane meal with a *spork* without being able to move my elbows more than 2 inches away from my rib cage lest I whack the guy next to me in the arm and send the contents of his fruit cup into his nice tie. True, if you can cash in enough frequent-flyer miles, have the money or did well on an upgrade, flying first class is another story. And believe me, I'm all for it.

As you consider your own comfort on the plane, be cognizant and considerate of the people around you. Don't bump or kick the seat in front of you and be careful when you stand up not to carelessly tug on the seat back of your fellow passengers. Keep your children behaving as politely and quietly as possible. Don't wear so much perfume or cologne that your fellow travelers hold their noses when they pass by.

First-class dreams, coach realities: Get comfortable — you're going to be here for a while

In first class, the ratio of bathrooms, flight attendants, leg room, bottom room, cushiness, complimentary champagne and spatial capacity to recline into a nearly horizontal position seems like it's about 8-to-1 of what it is in coach. But most of us fly coach, at least most of the time. Flying coach is a means to an end, but not always a comfortable one. So you have to provide yourself the comforts that you can. Fortunately, there are a lot of creative ways to do this.

How to keep your carry-on contents contented (and contained)

- Take a one-gallon resealable plastic bag and use it to store all the loose stuff you put in the seat pocket: paperback book, portable music device and CDs/tapes, pens, lip balm, gum, eyeglasses, miscellaneous toiletries. In other words, all the things that get loose, lost and left behind.

The other advantage of this system is that you can have essentials handy after you stow your personal bag. Keep in mind that some plane designs have limited storage space.

- Keep your briefcase or tote bag contents from getting scattered. Use resealable plastic bags to secure and organize individual toiletry items, pens and pencils, spare change, film — anything that could make a big mess if it spills when searched at security checkpoints or customs or if your bag contents should fall out.

- Plane travel can be rough on fragile items. Protect your valuables. Use custom-padded bags for valuable items such as personal computers, cameras, lenses, binoculars, eyeglasses. If you're traveling with breakable items, be sure you have a padded storage solution for each item. This is especially important now when bags are more likely to be looked through.

10 tips for staying comfortable

Surviving long flights is all about passing time and being as comfortable and content as possible. For the most part, plane travel is confining and, frankly, it can be pretty boring. Keeping your attention focused on something that interests you — or even just sleeping — is much better than staring at the headrest in front of you or looking down the aisle wondering when the meal cart will get to you. When waiting for plane food becomes a form of entertainment, you know you should have brought some reading material.

1. **Aisle or window — which is better?** The relative freedom of mobility in an aisle seat is hard to beat, especially when you're trying to make your way to the bathroom. Two things to watch out for in the aisle seat: your elbow, like when the food and beverage carts are being rolled past, and objects in the overhead bin (make sure it's securely shut before you buckle up). Ask to be assigned an aisle seat when you make your reservation or when you check in. However, if you plan to sleep most of the flight, you'd experience fewer disturbances in a window seat.

Tips for healthier flying experiences

What exactly causes jet lag? There's no one answer. Jet lag usually is caused by a combination of factors, many of which travelers actually have a fair amount of control over. Here are five good ways to take the jet and leave the lag:

1. Stay hydrated. Drink lots of water, preferably the noncarbonated, sodium-free variety.
2. Avoid alcohol. Alcohol consumption increases the effects of jet lag and fatigue.
3. Avoid caffeinated beverages.
4. Avoid salty foods.
5. Try to get a jump on the time zone. The time difference between your departure point and your destination can be a major contributing factor to jet lag. If you can gradually adjust your sleep and eating schedule to your destination's time zone before you go, it can make a big difference.

2. **Stretch out, if you can.** If you're not on a full plane, ask the flight attendant if you can move to a row where you can have an empty seat next to you or — better yet — three seats in a row. Remember: Some seat arms can be pivoted up and out of the way, making it easier to stretch out or lie down. Once they close the cabin doors, empty seats almost always are up for grabs. Don't be shy about asking.

3. **Wear socks and easy-to-remove shoes.** This can make your flight much more comfortable and give sore, tired feet a much-needed break. No offense, but if you have a foot odor problem, please ignore this tip.

4. **Wear comfortable-fitting clothing.** Being buckled into a coach-class seat is confining enough without wearing tight clothing. Give yourself a break and dress as comfortably as possible. Since sitting still on a plane can get chilly, bring a sweater or a sweatshirt to keep you warm on the flight.

5. **Bring an in-flight toiletry kit** with extra contact lenses and fluid, moisturizer, toothbrush and toothpaste, personal hygiene items, medications you may require, headache remedy, chewing gum (for ear relief from altitude pressure) and antacids.

6. **Earplugs.** Block unwanted noise so you can sleep, work or read in peace.

7. **Eye shades.** Block unwanted daylight or cabin light so you can sleep.

8. **Inflatable neck pillow.** Essential for long flights. I recommend *inflatable* neck pillows because they're extra light and portable, and it's easy to adjust their bulk and flexibility by adding or releasing air as needed. The great advantage of a neck pillow is that it allows you to relax or sleep in an upright or partially reclined position without getting a neck kink.

9. **Bring good reading material.** Reading is an excellent way to kill time in airports, in lines and on the plane.

10. **Bring your own bottled water and nutritious snacks.** Keep yourself hydrated and have a good, nutritious backup meal plan in case you don't like what they serve or you find yourself hungry on a snack-only flight. Remember: If you have special dietary needs or restrictions (vegetarian, diabetic, low sodium), you can request special meals when making your reservations (at least 24 hours in advance of your flight). You may have read about the possibility of developing deep vein thrombosis (clots in the leg veins) connected to air travel. While the risk exists, you can do a few simple things to

minimize your risk. Wear comfortable clothing, avoid staying in the same position, especially with your legs crossed, exercise and stretch your legs while seated, stretch or stand up every hour (unless the flight crew has restricted movement).

And look for the headrests you'll find on some newer planes. They have side panels you can adjust to keep your head upright when you drift off to sleep. They're very comfortable.

In-flight safety and security tips

- People who fly a lot often tend to tune out the cabin crew or video presentation on aircraft safety. Not a good idea. Certain safety features and emergency exit locations can vary from aircraft to aircraft. Pay attention. Read the safety card in the seat pocket in front of you. And always keep your seatbelt fastened while you're in your seat. You just never know when you might encounter unexpected turbulence in flight — even when the "fasten seatbelt" sign is off.

- Know where the emergency exits are located on the plane — the ones in front of you *and* the ones behind you. Count the number of seat rows to the emergency exits in both directions. Why? Should you need to make an emergency exit from the plane in conditions where visibility is bad, you'll know how far you are from the emergency exit in either direction by feeling the seat headrests as you exit up the aisle. Also, if you count the seat rows, you'll know which exit is the closest to your seat if it's not readily apparent on sight.

- In the event of an emergency evacuation, do *not* try to bring your belongings with you. This slows down evacuation procedures and wastes valuable time and evacuation space in the aisles.

- Never leave your wallet, purse, ticket or other valuables behind when you go to the restroom. If you have a laptop with you, you can ask a crew member or a trustworthy passenger to keep an eye on it while you go to the restroom.

- Never leave valuables unattended in a carry-on bag or tote bag.

- Keep important documentation and methods of payment in a security wallet or money belt when you're traveling. For maximum security wallet comfort, wear it under your pants or skirt waistband but over your tucked-in shirt. This prevents chafing, which sometimes can be aggravated when you're wearing a seatbelt.

- If you booked your flight through a travel agent, check with the agent for the latest airline and security news.

Children flying alone

While most airlines still allow children over the age of 5 to fly by themselves, the terms and restrictions are tightening up because of liability issues. There were two cases where an airline lost track of a child temporarily; in one of those cases the child ended up flying to the wrong city. Obviously, nobody wants this to happen.

Some airlines allow unaccompanied minors only on nonstop flights. Typically, airlines allow unaccompanied minors ages 5-8 on nonstop flights, and ages 8-11 on connecting flights. Some airlines consider children ages 12-14 traveling alone as unaccompanied. Millions of unaccompanied minors fly every year and, though they're being more cautious about the terms, airlines certainly don't discourage this passenger market. But they do charge extra.

Fees for unaccompanied minors on domestic flights range from $25 to $75 each way on nonstop flights or for each leg of a connecting flight. For international flights, the fee can be $100 each way or each leg. Check with your travel agent or airline on the rules of travel for unaccompanied minors.

Make sure your child is prepared for the flight. Finances aside, make sure your child, whatever the age, is prepared for a solo flight. Pack snacks, bottled water, games, books, comfortable clothes and anything else you can think of to make their flight an enjoyable experience. And make sure they have some spending or emergency money. Meet the airline employee responsible for them and escorting them to the person meeting them.

Most importantly, be sure your kids know how to contact you (they should have all important contact information in writing and on their person), where to find help if they need it, and make sure they're comfortable being on the plane by themselves. If it's their first time flying, explain how takeoffs and landings feel, what the plane does and what they can expect to experience.

You'll need your ID to bring your child to the gate and to help them with pre-boarding, and the person on the other end who is meeting your child also will need proper ID. And remember to arrive at the airport at least an hour earlier than you normally would in order to fill out all the necessary paperwork. Always know your airline's guidelines for children flying alone and comply with them to the letter.

CHAPTER 13

CAR TRAVEL

*Road tips for road trips,
including info and tips
about rental cars*

DRIVING
Three fundamental priorities

It doesn't matter whether you're traveling in a car by yourself, as a couple or as a family. There are three fundamental priorities. They are:

Safety — Organization — Comfort

Safety first, naturally. Organization comes second, not because it's more important than comfort, but because good organization contributes so much to making things both safer and more comfortable. More on means and methods of organization and comfort in just a moment.

Safety tips

- Always buckle up. Boringly fundamental, right? Wrong. Fastening your seatbelt is the *first* thing you want to do and the *last thing* you want to undo when it comes to automotive safety. Nothing is more likely to protect you and yours from harm when you travel by car.

- Don't drive when you're tired. Use rest stops. Get out, walk around, get some fresh air, rest your eyes, take a breather, switch drivers, have a cup of coffee or a soft drink, or get a room for the night.

- Make sure the car is mechanically sound (especially brakes and tires). This means a lot more than making sure the oil is topped off and the engine is tuned before you go. Naturally, you don't want to have engine trouble on your trip. But whereas engine trouble is an inconvenience, it's generally not as dangerous as bad brakes or tires. Out on the freeway in a vehicle that's traveling at speeds of up to 70 mph (and carrying the additional weight of passengers and luggage), bad brakes or worn tires are a disaster waiting to happen. Make sure yours are in good condition before you go.

- Check road and weather conditions before you go. What's the weather like? Will you need traction tires or chains? Are there construction delays or traffic advisories en route? Thanks to the Internet, it has never been easier for motorists to find out if their path is clear. Check out these sites for starters:

  ✓ aaa.com — AAA's site includes weather and traffic conditions, road safety tips and tons of info for travelers.

  ✓ accutraffic.com — The URL says it all.

  ✓ accuweather.com — Ditto.

  ✓ fhwa.dot.gov or nhtsa.dot.gov

Common-sense safety tips every driver should know

- Use turn signals. It's amazing how many people treat turn signal use as an optional activity. It's not. Please use them.

- Drive with your lights on during the day, especially when you're traveling long distances on the highway. You can see just fine. What's the big deal? Driving with your headlights on during the day isn't so you can see better. It's so other drivers can see *you* better. It's safer.

- Know when (and when not) to use your high beams. High beams can increase your safety if you use them properly and decrease your safety when used improperly. They increase visibility distance for night driving. They make it easier to spot animals in the dark because they're more likely to reflect in their eyes than low beams. However, it's rude and unsafe to have your high beams on when there is a car coming toward you in the oncoming lane or when there's a car in front of you on the road. High beams (even from far away) can be blinding when they're pointing at you. Give fellow drivers a break. Also, high beams actually can *reduce* visibility in heavy snow and fog, which reflect the light back into your eyes.

- Don't tailgate. Tailgating is dangerous for two reasons. One, if the person in front of you stops suddenly, you both could be injured or killed — especially if you're traveling at freeway speeds (and, legally, when you hit somebody from behind, it's *your* fault — even if they hit the brakes suddenly). Two, tailgating makes people mad. Nobody likes to have somebody riding their bumper. There's enough road rage in the world already. Let's all commit to backing off a bit. A minimum of two seconds of following time/distance is good.

- Don't cut people off. There are two ways to cut people off — both of them dangerous and just plain stupid. One is created with an abrupt lane change (usually executed without a turn signal) on the freeway. The second happens when someone suddenly pulls out in front of an oncoming vehicle from a side street or stop sign. *Not* doing these things also helps reduce incidents of road rage.

- A cell phone can be a great security feature (more on that in just a moment), but it also can be a source of distraction and danger. In some states, it's illegal to use a phone while driving. Using a cell phone in a moving vehicle takes your eyes off the road and at least one hand off the wheel. Worse, it takes your mind off your driving. According to AAA, there's no documented evidence that *hands-free* cell phones are any less dangerous than the handheld kind. Why is that? Because drivers get distracted by the conversation as much or more than they do by operating the cell phone itself. If you must use a cell phone while driving, make sure you're familiar with its features, keep the conversation short, have someone else dial for you if possible, and keep your eyes on the road and your mind on your driving. Never use a cell phone in challenging driving conditions such as bad weather or heavy city traffic.

- Don't just look ahead when you drive. Continually monitor the situation in your rearview and side mirrors with quick glances. Be fully aware of your surroundings, not just the road ahead. Knowing where other cars are on the road helps you make better quick-reflex choices in hazardous situations. It also keeps your eyes active and helps prevent the drowsiness that comes with "zoning out" when you just stare at the road ahead.

Close encounters of the four-legged kind

- Be aware of signs that warn about animals — deer, livestock, elk crossings. Be especially careful at night, when reduced visibility means reduced response time.

- If you see an animal — especially deer — by the side of the road, slow down. Where there's one, there's generally more.

- Most animals are nocturnal. You need to be especially careful at dawn, dusk and at night.

- Never swerve violently or slam on the brakes for small animals. I know this sounds terrible, but it's much better to accidentally run over a chipmunk than to swerve into oncoming traffic or be rear-ended.

- If you do accidentally injure an animal, do not get out of your car and approach it. Wounded animals often will attack.

- If a collision with a larger animal is unavoidable, slow down as much as you can before the impact, but let off the brakes right before the car hits it. Sudden braking forces the front end of the vehicle down, making it more likely to send a struck animal into the windshield. This isn't a pleasant tip to contemplate having to use, but it could save your vehicle from additional damage.

- Pass with care. On the freeway, use the left lane only to pass. If you want to drive more slowly, stay in the right lane. On two-lane roads, never, ever pass on a hill, a curve, anywhere near an intersection or in any other conditions that compromise visibility and safety. If you can't see a clear stretch of road with enough distance to pass, don't risk it.

THE MECHANICS OF SAFETY: VEHICLE SAFETY TIPS

- Pull off the road whenever possible. Make it easy for other motorists to see your vehicle. Use emergency flashers — especially at night or in bad weather that makes visibility difficult. Use flares or warning reflectors, open the hood or tie a brightly colored bandanna to the antenna. Flares or triangles should be placed at least 10 feet behind the vehicle on the side of the car that is closest to the road. Of course, never use flares if you have any sort of gas leak or if there are any flammable materials nearby.

- If your car breaks down and you can't get it off the road, get everyone safely out of the vehicle and either stand on the road shoulder or a sidewalk away from traffic. If you have car trouble, your primary concern should be your own safety and the safety of your passengers.

- Know where your vehicle is. Look for freeway exit signs, milepost markers, street names and intersections, and landmarks — anything that will help an emergency road service person find your car.

- If you have a cell phone and can use it to call for help, the emergency road service operator will need to know the following: your cell phone number (or number where you can be reached), vehicle location, make, model, license plate number and state, your membership number and insurance information.

- Be sure to ask the emergency road service operator to give you an estimate of how long it will take for assistance to arrive. Road service can come very quickly, but in situations where other drivers also may be in need (bad weather, for example), it sometimes can take hours. Be prepared.

- When calling for assistance, be prepared to offer as much information as you know about why the vehicle has broken down. The more information you can give them at the outset, the better the service is likely to be.

- Make sure the emergency road service operator is aware of any special circumstances — for example, if you have more people with you than could ride with the tow truck driver.

Organizing for traveling with kids

- Have each child fill a "car" backpack with their favorite stuffed animal, games, CDs, headphones and other items. The bags can be kept at their feet or beside them.

- Place a cardboard box upside down between the kids in the back seat to act as a table and keep them apart.

- Don't pack crayons for hot-weather car trips or anytime your car may get hot. A better choice is colored pencils or washable markers.

- Should you feel threatened or harassed while you're waiting for help, call 911 on your cell phone or draw attention to yourself by honking the horn repeatedly and flashing the lights.

- If you must leave your vehicle, leave a note on the dashboard explaining what has happened and that you've gone for help.

- Try not to split up. If possible, stay with the vehicle while you wait for help (as long as it's out of harm's way).

- If you stay with the vehicle, keep the doors locked and the window cracked. Don't open the door or roll down the window for a stranger, even one who seems to be well-meaning. Be cautious of people who offer to help. It's better to ask them to call for help than to accept a ride from a stranger.

- If you call for help on a cell phone, stay off the phone once you've spoken with the emergency road service operator. Tow truck drivers generally carry cell phones these days, so if you're on the line when they call, it could delay or prevent them from finding you and your vehicle.

- Prevention is the best medicine. Most breakdowns occur when people run out of gas. Don't let your tank get much below halfway empty — especially if you're driving at night or through remote areas.

Vehicle safety checklist

The following should all be present, accounted for and in good working order before you hit the road. Note: Have a mechanic check anything you don't feel comfortable doing yourself.

- Brakes (including emergency/parking brake)

- Tires (including spare)
- Rearview and side mirrors
- All safety belts
- Headlights, tail and brake lights, reverse and instrument panel lights
- All fluids should be topped off to the specifications in your owner's manual: engine oil, radiator fluid, brake fluid, transmission fluid and windshield wiper fluid
- Windshield wipers
- Windshield should not be cracked or pocked
- Make sure there are no leaks: oil, gas, radiator fluid or air from the tires

Top 10 tire tips

1. Replace tires that are worn, going bald, have any ripped spots on them or are so old that the sidewalls are cracking.

2. Your spare tire should be in good condition and properly inflated, and you should have an easily accessible and fully functional tire-changing kit in your car: jack/jack handle, lug wrench, powerful waterproof flashlight, safety reflector, flare or light, some plastic sheeting (good for oily road surfaces or wet weather tire changing) and a can of flat tire fixer just in case you can't change your flat tire where you are.

3. Try never to change a tire on a dark road, the shoulder of a busy free-way or in a dangerous neighborhood if you can possibly help it. This is where cans of flat tire fixer come in handy. (Be sure you read the warning label.) Try to get your vehicle to a well-lit place where you either can change the tire or wait for road service in a safer environment.

4. If you have to change a tire by the side of the road, be extremely aware of oncoming traffic. Day or night, never assume you can be seen. Keep an eye out.

5. If you change your own tire on a trip, follow up by stopping at a service station and making sure that the tire pressure is OK and that the lug nuts are on tight. Service station personnel have hydraulic tools that secure lug nuts tighter than your average hand-operated lug wrench.

6. Don't drive long distances on undersized spare tires. Some people call them "doughnuts," the thin, spare tires that come with a lot of newer cars. They can get you to a service station, but they don't have the traction or stability of full-size tires, and they're definitely not in it for the long haul.

7. Read your vehicle's owner's manual. Know what your tire air pressure should be. Buy a tire pressure gauge and know how to use it so you can check your tires at filling stations. If you're not comfortable with this task — and that's certainly OK, many people aren't — that's why there are full-service gas stations in the world.

8. Make sure you've not only got the right tires on your car (all-weather, snow tires, whatever's appropriate for the environment you're driving through), but also check with your mechanic and be sure to have them rotated and balanced if they need to be before you set out on your trip.

9. If you do have a "blowout" (a sudden loss of tire pressure caused by hitting bumps, potholes or train tracks too fast or a sudden puncture or tear in the tire), *do not slam on the brakes.* Especially at freeway speeds. It may be your first instinct but resist it. Slamming on the brakes can cause the vehicle to roll or skid out of control. If you have blowout, keep a firm, two-handed grip on the steering wheel, check for traffic before you slow down or change lanes abruptly, take your foot off the gas when it's safe to do so, brake very carefully and pull the car off the road as soon as you possibly can. It's preferable not to drive on a flat or a rim, but it's always better than having an accident.

You and the kids can enjoy these games

Auto Bingo. The one I like best allows you to slide the door on the gamepiece over the picture of the car, stop sign, horse or other illustration on the gamecard. It's great to play with all ages and there are no pieces to lose.

Play the "I'm going to Grandma's or Aunt Nellie's house and I packed a _____." Each item must start with A, B, C and so on through the alphabet. Each person has to add an item and then repeat all the items said previously.

Another favorite is **I Spy.** In this game you pick something that everyone can see and start giving hints about it. "It's blue. It's square," and so on until someone guesses what you're talking about.

And don't forget that all-time favorite: Find license plates for all 50 states.

10. If your tires are under warranty, make sure you bring the necessary paperwork should you need to replace them. Many tire company chain outlets do have your information on file but, as with so many things in the world of travel, it helps to have it on paper, too. If your tires are no longer under warranty, replace them.

Children and safety seats

- Kids under the age of 12 shouldn't ride in the front passenger seat, especially if your car is equipped with a front passenger air bag. Air bags can save adult lives, but the force and location of their sudden deployment can injure or kill small children.

- Never let children who are in booster seats or who use regular seatbelts put the shoulder strap behind their back.

- Set a good example. No matter how much you tell your kids to buckle up, if you don't do it, that's the lesson that will really sink in.

Ways to know if your child's ready for a regular seatbelt

1. They can sit all the way against the seat back and, without having to slouch, can bend their knees comfortably over the edge of the seat.

2. The lap belt fits snug across the top of their thighs and doesn't ride up on their stomach.

3. The shoulder belt should be able to come across their shoulder and rib cage, *not* their neck.

4. They can sit in reasonable comfort with the belt on for the duration of the trip.

Guidelines for a child's safety seat

Age and weight	1 year and younger and under 20 pounds
Safety seat required	rear-facing infant seat
Location	back seat
Age and weight	1-4 years old and 20-40 pounds
Safety seat required	forward-facing child seat
Location	back seat
Age and weight	4-8 years old and more than 40 pounds
Safety seat required	booster seat used with car's lap/shoulder belt
Location	back seat

Safety seats, air bags and children

For good information about travel safety in general and information about safety seats and air bags that every parent needs to know, check out the National Highway Traffic Safety Administration's website at nhtsa.dot.gov or AAA's website at aaa.com. For more family travel tips, as well as a look at some of the lighter aspects of family travel, see Chapter 9.

Personal safety and security tips for motorists

- My No. 1 tip for women traveling by car alone: Bring a cell phone with you. Even if you don't care for everyday cell phone use, it's still a good idea to travel with one in case of emergencies.

- Plan your route ahead of time. To maximize personal security, stick to well-lit, well-traveled roads.

- Let the people at your destination know what time they can expect you to arrive, where you'll be staying along the way and how they can contact you.

- Always keep your car doors locked when you drive and when you stop.

- If you think someone is following you, drive to the nearest police station, highway patrol station, fire station or (open) gas station.

- Be suspicious if someone bumps into your car or motions you to pull over as though there were something wrong with your car. Signal them to follow you, then drive to a police station or any of the other places listed in the tip directly above this one. Don't automatically get out of your car to inspect the damage.

- When you park at destination sites or in the city, try not to advertise that you're a tourist. Don't leave maps and brochures on the dashboard or seats. Never leave anything that a thief might want to steal in sight inside your vehicle.

- If you must leave anything of value in the car trunk (and this should only be done when you really have to), try to put it in there before you park at your destination. Even if you pull over a block or two *before* you park and place valuables in the trunk, it's better than doing it where you park.

- Whenever possible, park in well-lit places. Park where people can see your car, either in a public place or as close as possible to the parking lot attendant's booth.

- Never leave your car unlocked, even if you're just popping into the mini-mart for a bag of chips or a newspaper.

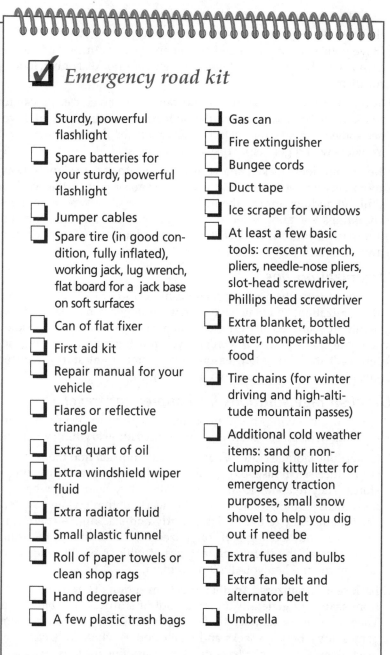

☑ *Emergency road kit*

- ☐ Sturdy, powerful flashlight
- ☐ Spare batteries for your sturdy, powerful flashlight
- ☐ Jumper cables
- ☐ Spare tire (in good condition, fully inflated), working jack, lug wrench, flat board for a jack base on soft surfaces
- ☐ Can of flat fixer
- ☐ First aid kit
- ☐ Repair manual for your vehicle
- ☐ Flares or reflective triangle
- ☐ Extra quart of oil
- ☐ Extra windshield wiper fluid
- ☐ Extra radiator fluid
- ☐ Small plastic funnel
- ☐ Roll of paper towels or clean shop rags
- ☐ Hand degreaser
- ☐ A few plastic trash bags

- ☐ Gas can
- ☐ Fire extinguisher
- ☐ Bungee cords
- ☐ Duct tape
- ☐ Ice scraper for windows
- ☐ At least a few basic tools: crescent wrench, pliers, needle-nose pliers, slot-head screwdriver, Phillips head screwdriver
- ☐ Extra blanket, bottled water, nonperishable food
- ☐ Tire chains (for winter driving and high-altitude mountain passes)
- ☐ Additional cold weather items: sand or non-clumping kitty litter for emergency traction purposes, small snow shovel to help you dig out if need be
- ☐ Extra fuses and bulbs
- ☐ Extra fan belt and alternator belt
- ☐ Umbrella

- Back into parking spaces whenever you can; it makes exiting them quicker and safer.

- Have your keys in your hand as you approach your parked vehicle. Don't stand by the car fumbling through your pockets or bag looking for them.

- You're most at risk getting in and out of your vehicle. Be careful. Look in the back seat and on the floor before getting back in. If you see someone suspicious standing near your car, don't try to get in it. Walk away and get help. Trust your instincts.

- Keep your doors locked and your windows up at stop signals. Leave room between yourself and the car in front of you so that you can pull out and get around them if you have to. Be aware of your surroundings — and especially the people in them. If someone approaches your vehicle in a threatening or suspicious manner, drive away as quickly as you safely can.

Organization tips

There's actually a pretty significant relationship between safety and organization. You may have a terrific emergency road kit, but if the contents are scattered all over the trunk of your car and you don't know where your flashlight is, it won't do you much good in an emergency. Safety isn't the only good reason to keep important stuff organized. Convenience and sanity are two more biggies.

Great storage solutions for happier car travel

It's an old saying, but a good one, "a place for everything and everything in its place." Here are some places for everything you bring:

1. Collapsible storage crates. They're terrific. You can find them in most stores that sell household goods and places such as office supply stores. They're about $5 to $10 per crate. They hold stuff when you need them to; they collapse down to nearly nothing when you don't need them. They're lightweight, sturdy and stackable — perfect for car travel and keeping stuff organized but accessible in the trunk. They have all the storage advantages of milk crates, but they don't take up room when you don't need them.

2. Back-seat organizers. Another great invention. They hang off the front seats and generally are made out of sturdy, washable canvas. They're great for families traveling with children, as you can store games, toys, books, snacks and water bottles where kids can easily reach them. Or you can have one for adults, one for kids.

3. Collapsible cooler. Very handy. Same idea as the collapsible crates. Coolers are great for car travel, but why should they take up space when you aren't using them? They don't have to. They can be especially handy for use in the hotel room. Fill them with ice and use them for an in-room fridge.

4. Bungee cords. I recommend always bringing three or four bungee cords of different lengths with you on road trips. They come in handy for so many things. They keep luggage and crates from shifting, you can secure toolboxes and other loose items in the trunk, and should you have trouble with a trunk or hood latch, a sturdy bungee cord can secure them shut until you can get to a repair shop.

5. Plain, old-fashioned plastic garbage bags. For laundry, wet clothes or bathing suits and — radical idea — *garbage*. And don't forget the ever-popular resealable Ziploc bag. Useful for keeping stuff organized, spare fuses dry, loose coins, or storing leftovers in your car cooler. Always have a couple on hand.

For more tips on being organized when you travel, see Chapters 7 through 11 for packing tips, more family travel and pre-departure tips.

Comfort tips

• Always take a water bottle in the car, preferably one per person. Staying hydrated helps prevent fatigue and grumpiness.

• Don't pass up rest stops, especially if you're traveling with kids.

• Stop regularly and get fresh air. Move around, get the blood flowing and get the kinks out.

• Wear comfortable clothing on long car trips. Loose-fitting clothes made from natural fibers are best.

• Bring pillows and blankets for more comfortable sleeping in the car.

• Always bring a pair of sunglasses. Glare isn't just annoying, it causes driver fatigue.

• Try to avoid subsisting on drive-through fast food. Good nutrition is important on long road trips. Most fast food is very high in fat and salt, and both those ingredients contribute to fatigue and stress. Don't just fill up when you eat on the road, get good nourishment.

• Bring interesting things to listen to. Whether you like the news from Lake Wobegon, Jimi Hendrix, the playoffs or books on tape, make sure you've got something interesting to listen to in the car. Boredom is a form of discomfort, too. This is a good way to prevent it.

Places to go, things to do, things to see

Sometimes a car trip is just a car trip, and you need to get on the interstate and go from one dot on the map to another as quickly as you can. Sometimes a car trip is a road trip, a deliberate experiment in finding interesting and fun things along the way, even if they're a little bit out of the way. The good news is, there are tons of wonderful places to visit and things to do and see that won't break your budget. Here are some ways to find them:

- Chambers of commerce. Almost every town and city in the United States has their own chamber of commerce, and most of them have their own websites. (Pick a place, do a key word search on any city name followed by the words "chamber" and "commerce.") Chambers of commerce are de facto showcases for any local area, and they can give you lots of good ideas about things to do and see along the way.

- State tourism offices. These basically are the statewide equivalents of a chamber of commerce. Every state has its own tourism office with accompanying website and toll-free number. To find them, go to tourstates.com, the official website of the National Council of State Tourism Directors, with listings for all 50 states.

Teach your kids how to read maps

- It gets them involved in the trip and their surroundings.
- It improves their reading skills.
- It teaches them geography in a way that's interesting and fun for them (and you).
- It keeps them occupied and helps pass time during the trip.
- When they get older, they actually can help you navigate.
- It's a physics lesson in the relationship between time, distance and speed.

Caution: It also can make them throw up. I don't mean to be graphic, but some people definitely do get nauseous reading in a moving vehicle. If your children are included among these people, then obviously it's better to teach them their map-reading skills at rest stops, meal stops and filling stations.

Navigation tips

- Always bring a good, up-to-date map or road atlas on your trip. If you're a AAA member, you can get free, current state maps at their travel centers across North America.

- Use a highlighter to mark your route on the map — especially if you're traveling alone. It can prevent a lot of fumbling with the map and having to relocate the same route again and again, and it makes it easy to take a quick glance at a map without driving off the road. If you're traveling with children, it helps them keep track of your route and gets them involved in the trip and learning how to read maps.

- Travel with a compass. We all get so used to maps, road signs and gas station directions that we sometimes forget that what we really need to know sometimes is as simple as "which way is north?"

RENTAL CAR TIPS

Rental cars offer great conveniences for travelers, but obtaining one can be a bit of a maze. Sometimes just figuring out the actual bottom-line daily rate can seem like the search for the Loch Ness monster. Take heart: A little bit of key information can take you a long way. Here are some tips for getting a rental without "going mental":

Tips for getting better rates

- Saturday is the best day to get a good price on a rental reservation. Why? Weekly rentals come back in droves on Friday evening, and

'Are we there yet?' Here's an idea

Before leaving for your trip, give each child a set amount of money. Depending on your judgement, between $5 and $20. Give them the money in singles. Let them know this is their spending money, but for every time they fight, complain or ask, "Are we there yet?" they must pay YOU $1.

It's amazing how well the strategy works and how tight the children hold onto THEIR spending money.

Sara E. Losito
Regional Manager, Field Member Services
Louisiana / Mississippi
Metairie, La.

weekend cancellations and no-shows start happening around the same time. Simple supply-and-demand economics, like if there are more cars available than there are demands for, you get a better rate.

- Look into weekend prices and specials versus weekday prices. Weekends usually are a better deal because the weekday rate generally is the more expensive business rate.

- Airport rental lots are convenient, but you often end up paying more for your rental car if you pick it up at the airport. Naturally, the demand for rental cars is greater at the airport. And rental car companies pay more for that real estate, so you do, too.

Keeping kids and parents happy en route

Friends and family members sometimes share some creative travel tips with me. Here are two from parents, for parents that I thought I'd pass along:

- Sometimes parents just need a bit of peace and quiet — especially in a car full of kids. A friend of mine, traveling with her two younger children, invented what she calls the "Quarters for Quiet Program," promising a quarter for every 15 minutes of quiet, per child. Naturally, this program works best on certain age groups. A suitcase full of cash won't keep an upset 2-year-old quiet, and older kids might play this game but it might have to be renamed "Dollars for Downtime." However, my friend reported that the kids thought it was a fun game, and she got 45 minutes of quiet from two kids for $1.50 — which she described with a laugh as "really good value for the money."

- An editor friend of mine used to save all of the free toys in cereal boxes before her kids were old enough to be able to read the cereal box labels and know they were in there. She'd collect them for months, and by the time the family's summer vacation rolled around, she'd have quite a collection of toys to work with. During long road trips, she'd give each of her kids a toy for every hour of good behavior. Not only did it work, it helped the family — on a tight budget in those days — travel happily and inexpensively.

- Know the *real* rate. Service and airport fees, state and local taxes, insurance fees, hidden charges . . . it all adds up. How are you supposed to figure out the *actual* rental rate? Here's how: ask, ask, ask. Ask lots of questions. Like hotels, rental cars are a favorite revenue source for state and local governments, which add additional taxes and fees to the tab to pay for municipal projects. When you reserve a rental car, make sure you get the total price, based on the taxes and fees (including airport fees) applicable at your pickup point.

- If you're a frequent user of a particular company, sign up for any advantage membership deals or discount clubs they have.

- If you try to get the least-expensive car, make sure it has enough room for you and your luggage. One advantage of reserving an economy-class rental car is that sometimes an upgrade to a midsize vehicle doesn't cost much (or anything) at all. Here's why: Most rental car companies have the bulk of their fleet in midsize vehicles. Economy cars usually are the first to be overbooked. If you reserve an economy car, it's not uncommon to get a no-extra-charge upgrade to midsize.

- Call the toll-free numbers and compare prices. Sometimes rental car companies will match or beat a quoted price if you throw one at them. But, again, make sure you know all the fees and taxes when you get quotes from any company.

- Ask your travel agent to assist you with finding the best rate.

Pickup

- Know where to pick up the car? When you make the reservation, ask where the rental lot is in relation to the terminal. Do you have to take a shuttle? If so, where do you pick it up? Do they have a desk in the terminal? And, if so, how late is it staffed? For non-airport pickups, get the address, directions and hours of operation ahead of time.

- Check the car thoroughly. Check windows for cracks, the body for dents and scratches, and the interior for stains or other damage. Have the rental company make a note of anything you find so you don't mistakenly get charged for it when you return the car. Make sure the car is what you wanted, that it's clean and is in good working order.

- Ask about a nonsmoking rental car, if you prefer it.

- Always have your driver's license and a major credit card.

- You must be at least 25 to rent a car, though some companies make exceptions — for a price. Under-age renters have to pay significant additional fees and insurance coverage. It might be cheaper to buy.

Drop-off

- Unless you agreed to the rental company's fuel plan, make sure you return the car with a full tank of gas. If they fill it, it generally will cost you a lot more than if you had done it on your own. Rental cars always have (or always *should* have) a full tank of gas when you pick them up. Generally speaking, it's less expensive to avoid their fuel plans, buy your own gas and return the vehicle with a full tank.

- If you have to catch a plane, leave plenty of time (at least an additional hour) when you're returning a rental car. Though most rental companies have made efforts to speed up the return process, you never know when you might be delayed. Even if they're quick to process your drop-off at the rental lot, you often have to wait for the rental company shuttle to the terminal, depending on the lot location.

- Save your original paperwork from when you picked the car up. Make sure the price you were quoted matches the charges on your bill. Ask them to explain any discrepancies.

- If you're returning a car to the airport, it may be a good idea to spend your last night at the airport hotel so you can drop off the car the night before your departure and not pay for the extra day. But, remember: Airport lodgings usually are more expensive than lodgings elsewhere. If the airport hotel is significantly more expensive than the money you'll save on returning the car early, it may not be worth it. Of course, staying at the airport the night before you leave can be convenient, and returning your car early can offset the cost.

- Get cars back on time. Most rental car companies base their rate on 24-hour increments from the time you pick up the car. So if you picked the car up at 9:30 a.m. on a Thursday and return it the next day at 11 a.m., you'll be charged for two days even though you only used the car for one 24-hour increment plus an hour and a half.

How much insurance do you need?

- Don't duplicate coverage. Check with your own insurance company and find out if they either cover you while you're in a rental car or if you can pay a small fee for supplemental insurance. If you're traveling on business, you may be covered through a corporate policy.

- Check with your credit card company to see if they offer additional coverage if you pay for a rental with their card. Many do.

Tips for international renting and driving

- If you're sharing a vehicle, always consider the amount of space you'll actually have. It's an increasingly common thing for two couples to go road tripping in Europe and rent one car so they can travel together while saving money on transportation. Great idea, unless you overpack. Rental cars generally are smaller in Europe, with limited secure storage space. Avoid inconvenience and conflict, and make sure all members of the traveling party discuss luggage limitations beforehand. One carry-on-size (22-inch) bag and one small tote or day bag apiece is advisable.

- Before renting a car overseas, check with your insurance company to see if you can purchase the necessary coverage through them. This can be a lot easier than trying to sort out insurance options in a foreign country. However, sometimes your credit card coverage or your own insurance policy may not be acceptable or recognized by the rental company. You may have to pay additional coverage.

- Be aware: Many foreign rental fleets have vehicles with manual transmissions. If you're not comfortable driving a stick, make sure you reserve an automatic. Also, be prepared for vehicles that only have kilometer-based speedometers.

- Have at least some idea of the driving conditions in the countries you will be visiting. Do people drive on the right or left side of the road? Road and driving conditions in many parts of the world are not up to North American standards. Have an idea of what you're getting into before you get behind the wheel in another country.

- Know the rules of the road in the country you'll be driving in. Here's a dandy website for those of you who'll be driving overseas: travlang.com/signs. This site explains European road signs, traffic laws and traffic customs, and has lots of good tips for driving overseas.

Keep in mind that gas is more expensive in most other countries than it is in the United States. Budget accordingly.

CHAPTER 14

TRAINS AND RAILS

Above and below

TAKING THE TRAIN

Train travel is like baseball: Most of the time, it's a civilized, leisurely activity. If you want something that happens in a hurry, you'd be better off at a Ping-Pong match or flying on the Concorde. When you choose to travel by train, you're not just purchasing transportation, you're purchasing an experience.

That used to be true of airplane travel in days past, but unless you're flying first class or taking a ride with a bush pilot into the Alaskan interior, it's rarely the case anymore. When you fly, you're paying to spend the least amount of time possible getting from point A to point B.

Then there's the train.

When you take the train, all the good stuff between point A and point B is precisely the point. If you're going to travel by rail, it's best not to be overly attached to a firm schedule. There are a lot of variables in train travel, and delays are not uncommon. But all things considered, the train still is an affordable, practical means of getting where you're going, especially in Europe.

AMTRAK

Amtrak has been on the brink of extinction more times than anyone can remember, which is pretty ridiculous when you stop to consider that it's our national passenger rail system, it serves 500 or more destinations, and some 20 million people use it every year. Amtrak or no, it's hard to imagine the United States without an interstate passenger train system. It's an important part of our history, and it's a great way to see the country — if you've got the time.

As of this writing, ridership is up, and Amtrak continues to offer a variety of accommodations, itineraries and money-saving rail passes. And it's a very inclusive method of travel. Amtrak can be a great way to go, whether you're by yourself, on a romantic getaway for two or traveling with children. It also can be a very comfortable mode of transportation for older travelers and travelers with disabilities. For more details, I recommend getting a copy of their *Access Amtrak* brochure.

Routes

Amtrak routes crisscross the country — north, south, east and west — traversing nearly every state in the continental United States. Currently, South Dakota and Maine are the only states in the lower 48 with no Amtrak service, though a new route is planned between Boston and Portland, Maine. OK, technically speaking, Amtrak doesn't cross into New Hampshire either. But the Vermonter runs along (you guessed it) the Vermont side of the Connecticut River from Brattleboro to White River Junction before heading up to Montreal.

Additional popular routes are the Acela Express (Boston to Washington, D.C.), the Crescent (New York City to New Orleans) and the Sunset Limited (Orlando, Fla., to New Orleans and Los Angeles).

Amtrak also connects to the Via Rail Canada system in the following places: Vancouver, British Columbia; Port Huron, Mich./Sarnia, Ontario; Toronto (by way of Buffalo and Niagara Falls); and Montreal, Quebec. And Amtrak sells a North American rail pass that gives you access to both Amtrak and Via Rail Canada lines. This creates interesting possibilities for North American train travelers.

Accommodations

Accommodations vary according to routes, but Amtrak offers a full range of options, from coach travel to deluxe bedroom sleepers with private baths. There also are family sleepers that accommodate up to two adults and two children, and wheelchair-accessible sleepers.

With reclining seats, extendable footrests and fold-down trays that can serve as a table or a little work desk, riding coach isn't bad. But it can get a little tiring on an extended journey. Needless to say, sleeping compartment accommodations are a train traveler's dream: privacy, enough space to sleep in a completely horizontal position and — in some cases — your own bathroom.

But they don't come cheap. Prices vary, but a standard sleeper usually is about twice the price of a coach ticket, and a deluxe sleeper can be triple the price of coach. Is it worth it? It depends on your budget, of course, but it's certainly a nice way to travel. And meals in the dining car are included when you travel by sleeper, so that is a factor to consider when deciding if you want to splurge.

As for meals on the train, Amtrak has dining cars with full table service and less-expensive cafe/snack cars. These can be nice treats, but I don't recommend relying on them exclusively if you can help it. If you're trying to keep costs down, it's a good idea to bring food with you.

Passes and discounts

Amtrak offers a number of rail passes and discounted fares for seniors, kids, and both high school and college students. AAA members also get a 10 percent discount on coach fares if they show their card when purchasing tickets.

An option that's definitely worth looking into is the North America rail pass, which is good for up to 30 consecutive days of travel in the United States and Canada, and covers 28,000 miles of Amtrak and Via Rail Canada lines. This pass requires at least one leg of travel in each country. For an additional fee, you also can upgrade all or part of your trip if you want to get a sleeper for a night or two.

Amtrak offers an increasing number of vacation packages that combine rail travel with air travel in case you're not up for a round-trip train ride. And last, but not least, look for good deals on off-season travel, with discounted fares that allow multiple stopovers.

Contact information

Needless to say, fares, pass programs and routes are subject to change. But if you're interested in taking a train trip, I recommend contacting your travel agent, checking out Amtrak's website at amtrak.com or phoning their (800) USA-Rail toll-free number and asking for a free copy of the *Amtrak Travel Planner* and the *Amtrak National Timetable*, which also are available from travel agents and at most train stations. These two publications or their website will be able to answer your questions.

VIA RAIL CANADA

If you love to travel by train, don't overlook Via Rail Canada. It has some terrific routes. Via also has some very good deals for seniors, students and parents traveling with children. And — attention, fellow Yankees — the exchange rate can make it a bargain.

Routes

Via Rail Canada has far-reaching routes that stretch from Prince Rupert on the Pacific coast of British Columbia, to Sydney, Nova Scotia and the Atlantic coast, some 6,000-plus kilometers to the east. Or you can hop off the trans-Canada line in Portage la Prairie, Manitoba, and catch a Via train north to Churchill on the shores of Hudson Bay. Via has some truly spectacular scenic rides, whether you're riding the rails along the St. Lawrence River in Quebec or crossing the Canadian Rockies where British Columbia's eastern border meets the western border of Alberta. Oh, Canada. Glorious? Indeed.

Accommodations

The accommodations are comparable but not identical to Amtrak's. The least-expensive option is economy class, but there's also Via 1 Class (basically business class, with extra-comfy seats and a meal included in the price of the ticket) and a variety of sleeper-class accommodations that vary from route to route.

As with Amtrak, Via has routes with full-service dining cars and cafe/snack cars. Again, I recommend bringing your own food to save money — though the occasional splurge in the dining car is a kick and feels very civilized.

Passes and discounts

Via has some very appealing discount programs and passes, all the more appealing for U.S. travelers because of the favorable exchange rate. Via's Canrail Pass gives you 12 days of unlimited economy-class travel within a 30-day period for around $400 (Canadian). That's a deal.

They also offer a Corridorpass, good for 10 days of travel in the Quebec City-Windsor corridor, including Toronto, Ottawa, Montreal, Quebec City and Niagara Falls, and a frequent traveler program for regulars.

The North America Rail Pass also is available through Via Rail Canada. Depending on the current exchange rate, you might want to comparison shop and see if you can get a better deal buying it through Via.

If you're planning travel via Via, make sure you check out their discount programs; they've got some goodies. Kids age 11 and under travel free in economy class as long as they're accompanied by an adult (one kid per adult). There also are discounted fares for seniors and youth (kids ages 12-17), and some really good bargains for students. Student discounts go as high as 35 percent and even 50 percent for regular trips between two frequently traveled points.

Here's a great deal for seniors (liberally defined by Via as age 60 and up): In addition to their standard 10 percent senior discount, Via also regularly offers free companion tickets to seniors for any age companion in *any* class of travel.

Naturally, discounts and passes are subject to change, but contact your travel agent, check out the Via Rail Canada website or call their toll-free number for the latest offers.

Contact information

Via has an excellent website (viarail.ca) that thoroughly details current accommodations, fares, discount programs and routes. You also can click on their scenic picture galleries from different routes if you really want to motivate yourself — or a travel partner — to get on board. Their number is toll-free at (888) VIA-RAIL, even if you're calling from the United States, and they're happy to send you brochures and schedules free of charge.

EURAIL

In America, train travel has become more of a novelty, an exception to the rule of the automobile. In Europe, it's more of a way of life or at least more of a *day-to-day* way of life. Trains are the most cost-effective, convenient way to see Europe if you're on a tight schedule — or if you're not on a tight schedule but want to cover a lot of ground. Either way, Eurail is the way to go. And, by and large, European trains run on time.

Routes

The European rail system is an extremely intricate network of lines and hubs that connect nearly every city and destination point on the Continent. This makes for an almost unlimited combination of travel possibilities, equally beneficial to travelers who like to plan everything down to the last detail and to those who prefer to wing it.

If you want to see Europe in a way that offers extraordinary flexibility, spontaneity and economy (and a steady stream of fascinating scenery), get a Eurail pass and ride the trains. (I'm using the term "Eurail pass" generically. There are a number of pass options.)

True, Eurail doesn't cover every destination — most of eastern Europe isn't covered, and Great Britain operates on its own system, BritRail — but it covers a lot, including passage on a number of connecting bus lines and ferry routes.

Accommodations

Eurail passes are good for unlimited first-class travel in participating countries. "First class" in Europe is comparable to coach in the United States, although generally a bit more comfortable. Reservations aren't required for traveling first class, but they're a good idea during peak travel seasons, and you'll need them for most of the high-speed trains. Otherwise, just get on the train and sit in the unreserved seat of your choice.

European train cars are clearly marked on the outside, near the doors, if they're first class, sleepers, smoking or nonsmoking. For an additional fee, passholders can upgrade to first- or second-class sleepers or a couchette, but reservations are required for these accommodations.

Sleeper rates vary according to the train and the trip's length, so check on the price when you make your reservation. Don't assume the last price you may have paid applies to all trains and routes.

Couchettes, for anyone unfamiliar with European trains, are compartments with bunks that accommodate four to six people. They're co-ed, and passengers sleep in their street clothes. Couchettes aren't as nice as the private sleepers, of course, but they're more affordable, they come with a pillow and blanket, and you can stretch out.

One thing: If you didn't reserve a couchette or sleeper, you often can upgrade en route. Ask the conductor if one is available and be prepared to pay cash in the local currency.

Speaking of stretching out, it's not out of the question when you're riding first class. First class on most European trains means train cars that are separated into six-seat compartments, each compartment having two rows of three seats that face each other. If you're not traveling on a full train, you usually can sleep in comfort, as each pair of facing seats can be folded down and converted into one fairly comfortable "bed" with enough room to stretch out and lie flat.

These converted seats generally are as comfortable as the couchette bunks — and cheaper, of course — but if the train starts to *fill* up, you might have to *sit* up and give back one seat.

As for meals, everything I said in the Amtrak and Via sections applies — except that train food in Europe almost always is more expensive and lower quality. Bring your own.

Passes and discounts

First things first: Make sure you purchase your Eurail pass *before* you go to Europe. Ironically, they're more difficult to get in Europe than in the United States.

There are Eurail passes to fit all sorts of different trips, budgets and time frames. The variations on the theme are too numerous to detail here (see contact information to get the latest), but the three main passes are the Eurailpass, the Eurail Selectpass and the Europass. All three passes allow you to configure different combinations of countries, travel days and lengths of time that the pass is good for.

• The Eurailpass is the most open-ended (and, therefore, the most expensive), allowing unlimited first-class travel in all 17 participating countries for as few as 15 consecutive days up to three consecutive months (with correspondingly higher fares, of course).

• The Eurail Selectpass is good for travelers with a more limited itinerary. It allows you to travel in any three adjoining countries of the 17 participating countries. This includes countries that are connected by participating ferry lines. So, for example, you could use the Selectpass to travel from Paris, France, to Brindisi, Italy, where you could catch the Blue Star ferry to Corfu, Greece.

• The Europass allows for unlimited first-class rail travel in France, Germany, Italy, Spain and Switzerland — the five most popular countries of the 17 that Eurail services.

That's a very basic overview. As noted, each of these passes can be configured in numerous different ways that allow for total spontaneity or completely planned travel. The best thing to do is to go over the latest brochure and timetables either by yourself or with a travel agent and figure out which pass — and which version of that pass — will work best for you.

The Eurail system can seem a little daunting at first, but the extraordinary flexibility of the pass options they offer can save you a lot of money, and it allows you to customize your rail pass to your trip.

Eurail also offers various "saver" pass options for two to five people. In a nutshell, you get a group rate. If you're traveling with friends or family members, this is an option you'll want to look into. Kids 4 and under travel free, but must sit on your lap if the train is full. Kids age 4-11 generally ride for half the adult fare, although there are exceptions. Eurail also offers a youth fare for second-class travel for those age 12-25. This would make a great graduation gift for college students completing their education.

Contact information

Eurail.com is the official Eurail site. I recommend raileurope.com, a much more functional and informative site for information about rail travel in Europe. Eurail doesn't have a toll-free number per se. Look for their brochures and timetables at participating travel agents. You can find more information about Eurail at AAA travel centers. If you're a first-time Eurail traveler, I strongly recommend talking to an experienced travel agent before buying a pass. An agent can help you sort through the options.

OTHER RAILS, OTHER PLACES

Eurail, Amtrak and Via Rail Canada are the focus of this chapter, but of course there are hundreds of rail systems all over the world. I can't even begin to do a quick overview of the world's railroads in this book, but if you're interested, I recommend checking out railserve.com. This is a fascinating site, with links to national and private railroad websites all over the world. Just type in the name of a country and search.

RAIL TIPS FOR RAIL TRIPS

In Europe

- Make sure you know which station your train leaves from. Many European cities have multiple stations.

- Be on time. The trains in Europe usually are.

- How do you buy, change or reserve a ticket at the ticket counter when you don't speak the language? There are several approaches to answering this question. Have your train number, time of departure and destination written down and hand the counter agent the piece of paper — it's a start. Use a highlighter and highlight the pertinent information on the train schedule and use that to help you at the counter. If all else fails, try to find somebody who speaks your language *and* the native tongue before getting in line. Usually there's somebody more than happy to help you.

- Double-check that you know where you're going ahead of time. Allow lots of time at the train station. Give yourself more time than you thought you'd need to get the right ticket and get yourself to the right track.

- If you have a second-class seat, don't sit in the first-class section. If you don't have a reserved seat, don't sit in one. European train conductors don't take kindly to people who "poach" seats. If you're caught in a couchette or a sleeper without a reservation, be prepared to be fined or taken off the train at the next stop.

- Always have your ticket or Eurail pass handy. With certain Eurail passes, you need to fill in the date you're traveling in the appropriate box on the pass (in pen) *before* the conductor comes around. Some conductors are casual about it, but others get upset and think you're trying to pull a fast one if you don't fill in the date by the time they check your pass.

- If you're sensitive to cigarette smoke, make sure you take note of the smoking/nonsmoking signs on the train cars. European smoking cars are *seriously* smoky.

Comfort, health and hygiene

- Sit facing in the direction the train is going, especially if you suffer any kind of motion sickness.

- Always bring good portable food with you on trains. Treat it like a picnic. Train food is expensive and sometimes can be hard to come by.

- Bring water with you on the train. Whether there's a cautionary sign or not, don't drink the water on tap in the train restrooms. Buying bottled water on trains is expensive, so bring your own, and use it when you're brushing your teeth, too.
- Always bring travel-size packages of tissues or extra toilet paper.
- Bring your own soap and washcloth or bandanna.
- Having packaged, portable sanitary wipes also is a good idea.
- Antibacterial handwash is great for train travel, in case there isn't running water available when you need it. Always have a back-up system for washing your hands without water.
- Once again, I recommend the standard-issue comfort kit, essential for long-distance train travel: eyeshades, inflatable neck pillow and earplugs. But don't let the eyeshades or earplugs compromise your security. Use them wisely and according to your own good judgment.
- Have a sweater, a sweatshirt, a scarf or even gloves readily accessible to keep you warm. Trains can get drafty and cold, especially at night.
- A blanket or a sarong can keep you warm and more secure — no easy access to your pockets or your day bag if you keep it looped through your arm and covered.

Luggage tips

- My No. 1 tip for traveling by train: travel light. Use wheeled luggage. If you're on the move, catching trains, getting on and off them, walking through stations and up and down stairs, you really have to consider how easy your luggage is to *schlep*.
- Never let your bag out of your sight at the station or on the train, unless you've stored it in a secure locker or at a luggage check area.
- Whenever possible, store your bag in the bin or the luggage rack in front of you (or ahead of you) so you can see it. Otherwise, people can get on and off the train behind you and take your bags.
- Use a portable, retractable cable lock (it costs about $15) to lock your bags to the luggage rack. Cable locks aren't invincible, but they do deter the grab-and-run type theft very effectively. Ideally, you don't want to let your luggage out of your sight; realistically, you sometimes have to because you have to go to other compartments to go to the bathroom, dining car, snack car or observation car. In such instances, take your valuables with you and lock up the rest as best you can. Lest this sound too cynical, let me just say that I've met a lot of great people on trains who have watched out for my luggage (and I for theirs).

- Most train stations offer secure baggage checks and pay lockers if you want to stow your luggage at the station and explore the town for a few hours before catching your next train. Have small amounts of the local currency in change and small bills handy for lockers and baggage check. But don't leave anything valuable or hard to replace — like your camera — in a locker or baggage check. Those items belong in your security wallet or day bag.

SUBWAY TIPS

So much for all of the *above.* What about the trains and tracks underground? There are incredible subway systems all over the world, so take advantage of them.

You easily can spend half an hour and many euros/lire/francs in the world's cabs trying to cover a distance a subway train would take you to in five minutes for an eighth of the cost. Practically everything in Paris, for example, has its own subway station: The Louvre, the Eiffel Tower, Notre Dame Cathedral and the Champs-Elysees. Even Franklin D. Roosevelt has his own (well-deserved) Metro stop. Subways can save you lots of time and money, but you need to know a few ground rules before going underground.

- When using the subway system in a new city, study before you leave home. Buy a guidebook, get a map and orient yourself. Most subway systems are fairly user-friendly and comprehensible, but it helps to brief yourself beforehand and pack a map when you go.
- Bring a compass with you. Big-city subway stations can be like labyrinths; a compass can help keep you on the right track.
- Most subway systems around the world have color-coordinated train lines/cars, making it easier if you don't speak the language.
- Look for information counters (clearly marked with a white "i" in a blue circle in most countries).
- Subway systems can be overwhelming — especially those that are new to you or in places where you don't speak the language. So take the subway when you have lots of time to get somewhere and find your way around.
- If you get off at the wrong stop, it's not a disaster. Wait a few minutes and catch the next train.
- Women: If you're nervous, always try to sit next to another woman.
- Smile and ask somebody for help. Have your subway map handy and point to where you're going if you need directions. Most people around the world are as friendly as you would be if a visitor asked

you for directions. You don't have to speak the language. However, I recommend the smaller pamphlet-style maps or guidebooks for orienting yourself, both in the city and the subway. You can look where you're going without advertising that you might not know where you are.

Subway security

- Don't stand close to the tracks on the platform, especially in crowds.
- Try never to stand alone on a subway platform.
- Keep your bag in front of you when you're waiting on a subway platform. If you're carrying a purse or a day bag over your shoulder, swing it around in front of you.
- If you have to use the restroom, don't leave your bag outside the stall. I'm amazed at how many people I see doing this.
- Don't hang your purse or your day bag on the hook on the inside stall door when you're using the restroom. This provides thieves with an all-too-common grab-and-run opportunity.
- If you're staying in an unfamiliar city, ask the hotel's concierge which subway lines and stops are most helpful for sightseeing and which are best avoided — especially after dark.
- Be prepared for up-close-and-personal contact on busy urban subways. But don't ever tolerate someone who uses that for an excuse to grope. Move away from them if you have to.
- If you have to stand when on the subway (and you often do), be sure you've got a good handhold. Subway trains constantly are coming to a stop from a high speed, lurching forward, suddenly going into turns that you can't see coming and so on. Get a grip and plant your feet apart a bit for good footing and to maximize your balance.
- Watch for signs that seats are for physically challenged people. Always give up your seat to someone who clearly needs it more than you do: an elderly man or woman, a pregnant woman, parents with young children or babes-in-arms, a person with any kind of disability or a local burdened with grocery bags, for instance. There are two ways to do this. You can ask if the individual would like your seat, but some people are too proud to take an offered seat that they otherwise might wish were available, and they'll decline. If this is a concern, you can strategically vacate the seat at the right moment when it will only be taken by the intended party. No muss, no fuss and good karma points for you, even if no one else noticed.

Finally, if you're traveling to any major urban center around the world and want to know about the subway system, look in the index of a destination-specific guidebook or get a map before you go.

Here's a hot tip for bargain-seekers: subwaynavigator.com is a *fantastic* website where you can explore subway systems all over the world. Not only can you get information about different subways from Manhattan to Moscow, you actually can pick a country and enter individual subway *stops* in specific neighborhoods. There's no charge, so check it out.

Things to do while you're on the train

1. Read. I also recommend bringing a good portable reading light.
2. Listen to music with headphones.
3. Write letters, postcards and travel journals.
4. Talk to people. Trains are a great place to meet people, shoot the breeze and exchange information and stories with your fellow travelers.
5. Play games. Bring travel-size board games or a deck of cards with you. Have fun with your friends — or people you just met.
6. **Bonus round:** Do nothing at all. Stare out the window at the scenery and dream.

CHAPTER 15

LEAVE THE DRIVING TO THEM

*An ode to the joys
of motor coach travel
and an omnibus
of tips for the road*

FIRST STOP ON THE TOUR

Don't confuse a motor coach with just another bus

Here's the best tip I know about bus travel: Never spend the night on a bus if you can possibly avoid it. No disrespect to buses, mind you. They're a very economical means of transport. They can be extremely convenient for short trips, mass transit and connecting legs along the way. However, sleeping on them isn't fun, and I recommend avoiding long hauls on the bus if you can.

But as I said in Chapter 2, there's a big difference between buses and motor coaches tours. Many travelers don't know this, and so they automatically eliminate a convenient, comfortable and fun source of transportation that might be perfect for their trip. Some travelers think coach tours are just for the older crowd, but that's a misconception. Coach tours come in all shapes, sizes, durations and destinations.

Put me in coach. Varoom! (with a view)

Sure, it might look like a bus, but check your preconceptions at the door. Look inside: Coaches are much more comfortable than your average interstate bus. They have panoramic windows to maximize your view, the seats are very spacious and cushy, and the bathrooms are deluxe; at least by bus standards anyway. Motor coaches are luxurious, climate-controlled and designed for maximum comfort even on long hauls.

Common interests, uncommonly good times

The organizing principle of the coach tour is that it gathers together a group of leisure travelers with common interests and helps them have a good time, see the sights and learn a lot about their destination in the course of a guided tour — whether it's a first class, eight-day autumn colors tour of New England or a three-hour sightseeing tour of Copenhagen.

Coach tours can be great for young people and singles, as well as couples and older people (single or not). And they're a fine resource for travelers who have a lot of interest in exploring but are new to a particular city, region or country, don't know their way around and maybe feel a bit nervous about striking out on their own.

The coach offers the traveler comfortable transportation, the security of traveling in a group, drivers and guides who know the area, a chance to see the sites, and an opportunity to meet and talk with other travelers.

In foreign countries, coach travel definitely can take the edge off of culture shock without blunting your sense of adventure or fun. There are a lot of reasons why people love coach travel, which is why good coach tour operators offer so many different options in so many destinations all over the world.

Different strokes for different folks

Coach tours come in hundreds of different configurations, from hourlong excursions to see a beautiful Alaskan glacier, to daylong sightseeing tours in hundreds of cities around the world, to 30-day multi-country package tours of Europe that include lodging, meals, luggage handling, airport transportation and even air fare, if you like. You can tour national parks, see the leaves in New England in the fall or take a day trip to a famous museum. If you want to see it, there's probably a way to see it by coach.

Where should you start?

To get an idea of the scope of services, the range of prices and the diversity of coach tour trips, I highly recommend either getting information about motorcoach tours at your travel agent, the AAA travel center or online.

Why do so many people like coach tours?

Coach tours are fun, sociable, low-stress and informative — especially if you get a good tour guide. And, by and large, the tour guides and coach drivers are very knowledgeable, helpful, friendly and — often — just downright entertaining.

Some of them are really very gifted and resourceful: They've got games, they've got entertainment and many of them are just a fount of information about the places you're traveling through and to. The good tour guides make it very fun and can be a big part of why coach tours are so worthwhile.

Full package coach tours offer the opportunity to travel without having to worry about anything. They do the driving; lodgings and luggage are attended to and, depending on the package, some or all meals are prearranged. For a lot of travelers, coach tours are a relaxing, cost-effective way to get out and see the world. The "group activity" aspect of coach travel is especially appealing to many people, who enjoy the camaraderie, shared sightseeing experiences and feeling of security when traveling as part of a group.

'Honey, they shrunk the coach!'

Some people really like the *idea* behind coach tours, but they're not comfortable traveling in a large group or they're looking for a more intimate or specialized tour experience. No problem: The world's a big place — but your coach doesn't have to be. Many tour operators offer mini-bus or van tours for smaller groups. Ask your operator or travel agent before you go.

COACH TOUR TIPS

Luggage

One of the benefits of a coach tour is that they take care of your luggage, within certain limits. They transport it back and forth between your room and the coach, which saves a lot of wear and tear on you. And you don't have to tip bellmen — an expense that otherwise could really add up over the course of a long coach tour. The luggage-handling services offered on many package tours can be a great convenience, but here are a few tips to keep in mind:

- Most tour companies limit you to one small personal bag that you can bring on the coach and one larger travel bag that gets stored in the cargo hold. A typical travel bag weight limit is 60 pounds. You can bring an additional bag if you really need to, but extra bags (or extra weight in your one bag) cost extra. This cost isn't necessarily prohibitive; one tour company I'm familiar with charges $3 per day for an extra bag — but you should know that before you go. Always check your individual tour company's requirements.

- Identify your luggage clearly and give it a distinctive marking to help make sure your bag doesn't get mixed up with someone else's. A colorful ribbon, handle pompom or brightly colored tape all work well for this purpose.

- Even on a tour where baggage handling is included, it's a good idea to travel with wheeled luggage, just in case you end up in a situation where you do have to handle your own luggage, if only briefly.

- A tip for couples traveling together: Cross-pack a change of clothing in each other's bag. If one of your suitcases is lost or delayed, you'll still have a change of clothing.

- For additional tips about luggage, packing and how to pack for a two-week trip using only one suitcase, see Chapters 7 and 8.

Comforts and conveniences

- Make sure you have the following items to keep you comfortable on and off the coach: sunglasses, sunscreen, a good sun hat (with a big brim), comfortable walking shoes and clothing, some bottled water, a few portable snacks in case you get hungry between meal stops and a warm sweater or sweatshirt — even in summer (in case the air conditioning is a bit chillier than you'd prefer).

- One thing I love about coaches is the flip-down footrests on the seat in front of you. You find them on a lot of trains, as well. I only mention this because a lot of times, people don't even know they're there. But look for them on the seat in front of you. You can pivot them down and put your feet up, and it can make your trip a lot more comfortable — especially if you're doing a lot of walking around when you stop to see the sights.

- Bring a jacket or something to lean your head against to sleep against the window. Windows can be chilly or have moisture on them.

- And for you coach-tour travelers who may have skipped the chapter on air travel, here's a tip that's worth repeating because it works so well on the coach, too: Bring a gallon-size resealable plastic bag with you and put it in the seat pocket in front of you on the coach. Use it to hold everything you'd like to have handy in the seat pocket but wouldn't want to lose. This is an easy method for using the seat pocket without losing your stuff. And at the end of the day when you're ready to leave the coach, instead of fumbling around in the seat pocket trying to make sure you got everything, you just pull out one plastic bag and toss it in your tote bag, easy as pie.

- Here's a question people often ask: Who gets to sit up front? Almost everybody likes the seats up front with the best view, but who gets them? There's no one answer, but most tour guides are pretty democratic about the plum seats on the coach and encourage passengers to rotate in and out every time there's a stop along the way. Generally, these seats can't be reserved. (Sometimes they are used for people who have disabilities.) Everybody who wants a turn can have one, and nobody ends up squabbling over them.

What about tipping on a coach tour?

- On many package tours that include meal service, tips for the meals are included in the price of the trip, but you're encouraged to leave at least a small gratuity if the service is particularly good.

- Should you tip the coach driver or the tour guide? Yes, you should. How much? Well, that depends on the tour and the guide. If you're traveling by yourself and you take, say, a two-hour sightseeing tour, a $2 to $5 tip for a good tour guide is appropriate.

- As for multiday tours, I suggest tipping the tour guide $4 per person per day and tipping the driver $2.50 per person per day. On one hand, that's a reasonable amount if the service is really good and you can afford it. On the other hand, many people may find that a bit beyond their range — especially on longer tours. For a couple: $6.50 per day for a 30-day tour equals $390. Yikes. That's fair chunk of change. However...

- Good drivers and tour guides do indeed depend on tips for their livelihood, and they deserve to be rewarded for a job well done. Always try to budget in at least *some* tip money when you go on a tour. Consider this: Even a dollar a day per person for the tour guide and the driver is still a nice thank you, especially when it's delivered with a word of thanks. A dollar's not that much to part with, but if 20-30 passengers on a tour tip the guide or the driver that much, it adds up. Your dollar can make a difference.

- On some stops, you might take a tour with a tour guide who works for a particular museum or historic site. In such cases, a dollar tip is appropriate should you care to tip.

- When tipping tour guides and drivers, couples should remember to tip an amount that's appropriate for two people. A lot of couples will tip a dollar between them. It's better than not tipping, but it's not ideal.

- Finally, as with all forms of tipping, use your own good judgment. If a particular guide was really wonderful and you feel they deserve a bigger tip, give it to them if you can spare the extra. It's a nice way of saying "keep up the good work."

Miscellaneous

Be aware that, when you purchase a package coach tour, the tour company will send you a complete information packet detailing their specific policies. Always be certain to read this information thoroughly before you leave for your trip, and bring it with you on your travels in case you need it. If you have any questions, concerns or special requirements, let them know.

CHAPTER 16

CRUISE SHIP TRAVEL

Good tips for cruise ships

SHOULD YOU CHOOSE A CRUISE?

Cruise ship travel is a world of adventure all by itself — and one you could write an entire book about. So this is not an all-inclusive-absolutely-everything-you-need-to-know-about-cruise-ship-travel-down-to-the-last-detail chapter so much as an introduction and overview with accompanying tips and information for travelers who want to know more about cruising.

What's in it for you?

The short answer is a good time. Cruise ship travel is as varied as the hundreds of destinations you can cruise to around the world. It can be low budget and casual, incredibly deluxe and formal, a nonstop party or a long rest in the sun. You can take a three-day cruise to Victoria, British Columbia, or a monthlong sojourn to Australia and Asia, or take an around-the-world cruise for 90 days.

What can you do? As much or as little as you want

Cruise vacations also can be as active or as relaxed as you want them to be. If you don't feel like doing much or if you just want to kick back in a deck chair all day, read your book and look at the water, you can.

On the other hand, if you want to be active, the options are there: swimming, dancing, miniature golf, basketball, socializing at the bar and live entertainment. You even can go ice skating or indoor rock climbing on some cruise ships. The point is, you can do as much as you want to or as little as you want to, when you want to, *if* you want to.

And that's just on board.

Ship to shore

Cruise ships dock in some of the world's most beautiful ports: Sydney, Australia; Juneau, Alaska; Puerto Caldera, Costa Rica. And they usually dock right near the cultural and commercial center of city life, at the heart of where the action is at any given destination.

Many travelers feel cruises offer the best of all worlds: complete relaxation mixed in with exotic destinations, natural scenic beauty one day, the excitement of city life the next.

Bring the family

Cruise ship vacations can be great for family travel and a creative way to hold a family reunion. You can get together and nobody has to do the cooking and cleaning. And, while there are plenty of things you can do together on board, there also are lots of opportunities for everyone to go off and do their own thing without a conflict of interest.

It's a great way to have freedom of choice and also be close to people. Cruise ships are a good value for family travel, because you can get package deals and you know the price of your entire vacation up front (unless you go wild with the credit card when on board and in port).

It's taken care of

Another reason so many people love cruises is that everything's taken care of, which makes for a low-stress experience. A cruise ship offers food, lodging, transportation, entertainment and activities. Just add sun and scenery. You also experience the advantages of dealing with only one currency and unpacking only once.

There are many reasons why cruise ship travel might fit your vacation fantasies and your budget, but it's not all champagne and roses. You have to pick the cruise that's right for you, and you need to find a cruise ship company with a good health and safety record.

Let's start with finding the right cruise.

What are your priorities?

 Before you buy your ticket, sit down and make a list of your top priorities for selecting a cruise — the things that are most important to you. Start by writing down whatever comes to mind, then prioritize them in order of importance. Whatever makes the list can be a very helpful guideline for a travel agent trying to connect you with the right cruise.

Here, in no particular order, is a checklist of possible considerations that you can add to as you see fit:

- Food
- Entertainment
- Ports of call
- Peace and quiet
- Party life or night life
- Best price
- The luxury travel experience of a lifetime
- A formal environment
- A casual environment
- A short excursion
- A lengthy getaway
- Lots of activities
- A nice family-oriented cruise
- A romantic getaway
- Ship safety, sanitation, environmental record

WHEN YOU CHOOSE TO CRUISE

- If you're new to cruises, I highly recommend sitting down with a travel agent to help you sort through the options and come up with the trip (and the ship) that best fits your lifestyle, budget and destination interests. There's a lot to know, and this is an area where a travel agent can save you a lot of time and potential headaches.

- Get brochures from a bunch of different cruise lines. Put five of them in front of you and see which one jumps out at you or appeals to your lifestyle. If they don't seem to be talking to you, they probably aren't.

- When checking out cruise prices, make sure you know what's included and what isn't. Many first-timers forget that air fare to and from the port isn't always included in the price.

- When it comes to getting the cruise you want and the cabin you want, the early bird definitely gets the worm. Once you've made up your mind to go and have chosen a cruise, make your reservations as quickly as possible to ensure that you get the accommodations you desire.

- If you want to sample cruising without investing a lot of time or money, start with a three-day or four-day cruise and see if you like it.

Cruisin' cruisin' cruisin' on the river

 Several of the most intriguing cities and towns of the United States, Western Europe, Russia and China are positioned on major riverways. If you've been thinking about visiting these areas on a leisurely basis but don't want to spend your time trekking from one city or hotel to the next, perhaps a river cruise vacation might be just for you.

River cruises offer you the flexibility of visiting cities and towns as well as the peaceful countryside between the metropolitan areas. With the boat as your hotel, you have to unpack only once. And since it's like other cruise experiences, you still receive most of the same amenities, excellent meal service and interesting shore excursion choices to various sights along the way.

Jim Sweat
Managing Director
AAA Travel Agency Services
Tampa, Fla.

- Protect your trip: Pay for your tickets with a credit card, not cash. That way, if there's a problem with the ship or if the company goes out of business (it happens every once in awhile), you're not out the price of a ticket.

- To protect your investment, you should always consider trip insurance. This is especially true for older travelers who may have health concerns. Trip insurance can cover the price of your ticket if a medical problem prevents you from traveling.

- Consider choosing a cruise ship that docks in the United States, because these are the ships that have to comply with Coast Guard safety standards.

Ship shape? Before you cruise...surf (the Internet)

Travel agents are a good starting point for gathering the information you need. I also recommend comparing their advice with your own online research.

The two most important things to know about a cruise ship are:

1. Is it safe?

2. Is it sanitary?

Cruise ship tipping guide

 When you book a cruise, ask your travel agent or the cruise line company about the ship's policy regarding tips and gratuities. There's not an absolute, universal standard for all ships. Sometimes gratuities are included in the price of the ticket, but as a rule of thumb, gratuities are given to the staff on the last full night of the cruise. Most cruise lines will provide you with guidelines in your final documents.

Here's a rough guide for tipping ship personnel:

- Cabin or room steward: $2.50-$3.50 per person in the room per day
- Maitre d': This depends on the cruise line. Some suggest $1.50-$2 per person daily; others suggest a single $10-$20 gratuity, but only for a special service.
- Dining room waiter: $2.50-$3.50 per person daily
- Assistant waiter: $1.50-$2.50 per person daily
- Bus-help: $1-$2 per person daily

WHAT C.L.I.A. IS — AND WHY YOU SHOULD KNOW ABOUT IT

CLIA is an acronym for Cruise Lines International Associa-tion, an organization that represents 23 cruise lines, which comprise 95 percent of the North American cruise capacity. They have a great website at cruising.org. This site is the mother lode of cruise information: cruise line and ship profiles, cruise finder, vacation planner, tips, trips and ships galore. And *very* user friendly. CLIA also trains and certifies travel agents as "accredited" or "master cruise counselor," designations that indicate their extensive training and knowledge in helping clients plan a cruise vacation.

SAFETY

Want to know about ship safety? Ask the United States Coast Guard. The website psix.uscg.mil/vesselsearch.asp will take you to the United States Coast Guard Port State Information Exchange System. I know it's a mouthful, but it's not at all complicated once you get to the site. You can search for safety information about ships using all sorts of search criteria — including simply entering the name of the vessel and clicking on "Search."

SANITATION

For cruise ship sanitation reports, check out the Centers for Disease Control website at cdc.gov. On their home page, click on Health Topics, and then select Cruise Ships. You'll find information you need to know that won't turn up in cruise brochures.

Cruise ship Q&A

Q: What is (and isn't) included in the price?

A: Included: most meals, ship accommodations, ocean transportation, some beverages, gratuities (on some cruise lines) and most of the entertainment. Not included: air fare, transfers, shore excursions, alcoholic beverages, soft drinks, photos and any medical services you may require.

Q: Do you have to have a passport when you cruise?

A: You need your passport if your cruise begins or ends in a foreign port or you're taking a cruise around the world. For cruises originating from and returning to a port in the United States, you only need proof of citizenship. A passport is useful for this, of course, but you also can use your birth certificate or a copy of your birth certificate accompanied by a photo ID as proof of citizenship.

Q: How old do you have to be to cruise by yourself?

A: This depends on the cruise line. Generally, you have to be at least 25 years old if you're traveling by yourself. It's very important to let the cruise line or your travel agent know if you're under 25. Believe it or not, you can be denied boarding if you show up by yourself with a ticket and you're under 25. Denied boarding is treated the same as a "no show." Translation: You're out the price of a cruise.

Q: Will I get seasick?

A: For the majority of passengers, it's either not a problem or it's a problem that's easily dealt with. Almost all ships are designed with stabilizers that minimize side-to-side roll. If you do feel sick, there are several different remedies available, both medicinal (like Dramamine) and non-medicinal, and they usually do the trick.

Q: Which cabin would be best for me?

A: If you have to have a view of the water, you'll want an outside cabin with a balcony or at least an outside cabin with a porthole. However, if you're susceptible to seasickness, an inside cabin on a lower deck toward the middle of the ship is your best bet. The closer you are to the ship's center of gravity, the less motion you feel.

Q: Is there smoking on cruise ships?

A: There are designated smoking and nonsmoking areas. There are also cruise ships that are entirely nonsmoking.

Q: When is hurricane season?

A: June 1 through the end of November.

CHAPTER 17

TAXI TIPS
AND TACTICS

*How to catch a ride
without being taken for one*

Common-sense taxi tip: Be in control before you roll

From New York to Newark, L.A. to London, there's a universal truth about riding in taxis anywhere in the world: Either you're in charge or the driver is. And this relationship usually gets established at the beginning of the transaction — often before you even get in the cab. The cabbie may be driving, but you have to be the one who's in control.

Fortunately, there are some easy, low-key ways to do this. Taxi drivers have the wheels, but you've got the money. That's what's known as a balance of power. Hanging in the balance is the question: How will you get there, and how much will you pay?

FIVE SETS OF TAX TIPS AND TACTICS
Getting a cab — different means to an end

There's more than one way to catch a cab. You can call ahead, hail them from the curb or even reserve a ride online, if you prefer. Whatever your method of choice, here are some tips to consider when it's time to catch a ride:

- Call ahead when you can. Most companies take what they call pre-arranged time calls. If you don't actually reserve a cab, at least remember to leave yourself plenty of time to get where you're going. Call well in advance, especially on Friday and Saturday nights or during peak travel times.

- When you first arrive at the airport or the train station and you're looking for a cab, be wary of people who walk up, ask you if you need a cab, offer to take your bags and so on. Make sure you're dealing with a licensed cab driver before you start handing over bags or offering information.

- Taking this same principle a bit further, don't get in unmarked cars or any other questionable vehicle. Look for obvious taxi markings, working meters and clearly posted driver identification.

- If you're new to a city and nervous about hailing a cab, or simply don't want to deal with it yourself, you always can have the front desk at the hotel call you a cab.

- Always have a dollar or two handy if the doorman or someone else from the hotel gets you a cab. You really should tip the guy who gets you a cab. It's a small courtesy, but it's a good way to say thank you.

- Sometimes you'll see cab companies advertising "computerized dispatch." Is this really that convenient or helpful to you, the passenger? Yes, it is. Computerized dispatch means that a company's cabs are equipped with GPS (global positioning system). This gives the dispatcher a clear idea of where a cab is and how long it'll take it to get to you.

Dealing with drivers: the rights (and wrongs) of passage

- When you're telling the driver where to go, speak clearly and make sure they can hear you. Plastic partitions, traffic noise and language barriers can make it difficult for the driver to understand you.

The fine art of hailing a cab

For some people, hailing a cab is a fun exercise in being a self-assertive, independent urban traveler. Others find it intimidating and are very shy about raising their hand. For a lot of urban dwellers, it's a daily routine no more exciting than folding the laundry. Regardless, knowing how to hail a cab is a useful life skill. Here's how to do it:

- First, look for a cab that's in service. Look at the roof light or sign. If that's lit up so you can read the number, the cab is available. If the roof light or sign is off, the cab is occupied. Occupied doesn't necessarily mean it currently has a passenger inside. The driver could be on his way to a pickup or on the way home.

- Stand at the curb, in a spot where you can easily see the cabs and the drivers can easily spot you.

- When you see an available cab, raise your arm up and out, above your head at the 11 o'clock or 1 o'clock position and point. Make it a decisive, unambiguous gesture. You'll feel really good when the cab pulls over. Don't be afraid to give a holler or whistle. If you're one of those lucky people who can whistle loudly enough to get a cab driver's attention, that's a skill it would be a shame to waste.

In addition to raising your arm and making noise, eye contact can be very helpful. Sometimes a driver will give you a questioning look as if to say, "Are you trying to hail me or are you just stretching your arm." Look them in the eye, give them a nod or beckon them over. Hailing a cab really is good assertiveness training.

- It helps to have at least some idea of where you're going when telling a driver your destination. Most of them won't give you the runaround, but they may take a longer or more lucrative route if you don't seem to know the area well. Those portable, laminated city maps can be helpful. Sometimes just looking or acting like you're in familiar territory can help.
- Try to keep your bags with you, as opposed to putting them in the trunk.
- Make sure you get the name of the driver, the cab number and the cab company name in case you leave something in the cab.

If the driver is going too fast, and it's making you nervous, here's a simple but effective way of dealing with it: Tell him to slow down. Obvious, right? But it's amazing how many people don't feel like they should be back-seat drivers — even when they're in the back seat clenching their teeth.

- Always write down your destination's address and be prepared to show it to the driver if need be. Hotel postcards or matchbook covers from the hotel where you're staying are certain to have the hotel address on them. If you carry one with you, you'll have something to show the driver in case you forget the address.
- Wear your seatbelt in the cab. I don't know why so many people don't buckle up when they get in cabs, as if there were some sort of force field around them. There isn't.
- And finally, if you do need to file a complaint (or for that matter, pay a compliment to an exceptionally helpful or courteous driver), this is the information you'll need when you contact the cab company: the driver's name (look for his ID, usually on the dash near the glove compartment or up near the top of the windshield), the cab company's name, the cab number, date, time of day, trip origin and destination.

Reading the meter: fares and un-fares

- Watch the meter. Here's how cab meters work: When you get in the cab and tell the driver where to go, he starts the meter. There's an initial meter drop fee that varies from cab to cab but usually is around $2. A typical rate from there is around 40 cents for each quarter mile when the cab is moving or 40 cents for every minute and a half of traffic delays or waiting. Just make sure the meter's not set too high when you first get in the cab.
- Some cabs have a flat rate for specific trips (trips between downtown and the airport, for example). As just noted, taxi meters click off time spent in the cabs, not just miles. So a traffic jam on the way to the airport can add money to your fare. Flat rates can be a good deal.

- Beware the double-whammy scam. Here's how it works: You and a companion negotiate with a driver to establish a flat rate to go from, let's say, the airport or train station. An amount is agreed upon. When you get there, the driver tells you that you *each* owe the amount that you thought was for *both* of you. If your bags are in the trunk of the cab, it can make your negotiation a lot tougher.

What can you do? Argue with the driver; be obvious about writing down the license number of the cab or limo, or look for a cop (though most of them don't really care to sort out fare disputes). In this case, prevention is the best medicine. When a price is named, make sure it's agreed upon as the *total* fare for *both* parties.

Start with a lot of common sense

1. I always try to have a city map and calculate the route and distance from the airport. This gives me a head start with the driver as I have it in plain view; they know I'm aware of the driving time and general route. If the driver asks if this is my first time in the city, I usually answer with "I know my way around."

2. I make sure the driver understands my destination and knows how to get there before the cab leaves the airport. And I don't hesitate to tell him if something isn't right, before he drives for some distance with the meter running.

3. Know the rate of exchange on currency and have funds available in that currency *before* leaving the airport. If you know the rate of exchange, drivers will usually accept American currency if that's all you have.

4. In some countries you can hail a cab only from certain locations; it may be improper to whiste or try to hail one otherwise. Purchase a book about the country you're visiting and study the public transportation system; it could be cheaper or convenient to use buses, the subway or hotel transfer vans.

5. Pay the fare after exiting the cab and when you have all of your possessions in hand.

George Shaffer
AAA General Manager
Sunbury, Pa.

- You always can ask the driver to estimate the fare to a specific destination. A lot of times they have a pretty good idea.
- Many taxi companies offer an hourly rate, which can be a really good option if you have a lot of distance, time or stops to cover.
- Very few cab companies let you pay with a charge card, so don't count on it. Ask ahead of time. In a worst-case scenario, have the driver stop at an ATM and get some cash.

Arriving, paying and tipping — why small bills make a big difference

- Always keep small bills handy and easily accessible in an outside pocket so you don't have to dig through your security wallet. Smaller bills make it easier to tip and pay cabbies without having to wait for or count your change. Don't get your money belt out to pay for your fare.

Sharing a cab — rules for the road

Cab sharing can be a great way to save money, but there are a few things to know about how it works. The following tips are not foolproof guarantees for every taxi in the world's thousands of taxi fleets. But generally speaking, here are the rules:

- If a group takes a cab to a single destination, that's considered one fare.
- If there are separate drop-off points, with each passenger paying for himself or herself, the driver gets to reset the meter (and gets the initial meter drop fee again — usually about $2), unless one passenger pays for everyone. This is a fair system, because the cab driver's time is money. Extra stops, payment transactions and unloading all take extra time and effort.
- If you're trying to catch one cab with a group of people, keep in mind it's illegal for cab drivers to give rides to any more passengers than he has seatbelts for in his cab.
- Whatever you do, whether there's one drop-off point or several, if you're traveling by cab in a group, figure out who's going to pay what *before* you get in the cab. If that's not possible, at least take care of it before you get to your destination. No working cabbie has five minutes to spare while a group of people try to figure out fare payment.

- Start calculating the tip in your head well in advance.
- Make sure the driver stops the meter as soon as he stops at your final destination. Only pay the amount on the meter (plus whatever you wish to tip). Generally speaking, there are no added charges for handling bags or packages.
- Get a receipt. Most taxi receipts have the cab number on them, which can be helpful if you accidentally leave something behind in the taxi.

    And last but not least...

How to accidentally leave something in a cab, never see it again and be really annoyed with yourself (and other things to keep in mind when exiting a cab)

- Relax. You're there. The meter's turned off. Did you get everything out of the cab? Everything that was in the trunk and stowed on the floor? If not, remember this: Unless you're late for the plane, there's no rush. When the cab stops at the final destination, so does the meter. And if it doesn't? Remind the driver. If you can, keep your purse, briefcase and bags next to you or on your lap. That way, you have a better chance of taking it with you. Remember: Cab companies take no responsibility for items left in the cab.
- And finally, be careful exiting cabs. Watch for traffic. Always get out on the curbside of the cab whenever possible.

Are you sure you need a cab? Alternate wheels

- Sometimes a limo actually can be cheaper than a cab or at least a comparable alternative — especially from the airport to downtown. If everyone is lining up for cabs, and the limos are just sitting there, sometimes you can play let's make a deal with a limo driver for a decent flat rate for a ride. And if you've got a couple of people, it really can defray the cost.

The scuttlebutt on the shuttle

- Shuttles can be an inexpensive alternative to cabs, but always consider the value of your time when you are considering the shuttle option. There are exceptions to nearly every rule, of course, but I've found this formula to be a fairly reliable gauge when comparing taxis and shuttles. Shuttles cost you about half the money, but twice the time that cabs do.
- Try to avoid buying a shuttle ticket from someone standing on the curb. Sometimes, especially when you arrive late, that's your only option, but be cautious. Try to buy your ticket at the counter in the airport whenever possible.

• Always watch where they put your luggage on the shuttle van. Keep an eye on it. This is another place where cable locks really can come in handy for keeping several bags safely tethered together. Cable-lock them together in the shuttle van storage area, preferably running the cable through something attached to the van, such as one of the back-seat legs. This way, when they're taking everybody else's bags out at other stops, they don't accidentally take your bag off at the wrong place.

How much should you tip a cab driver?

 That depends on the length of the ride and the quality of the service. One rule of thumb: $1-$5 per trip. Some people tip 15-20 percent of the fare. Other people think that a 15-20 percent tip is outrageously generous.

CHAPTER 18

THE BORDER

*Lines and crossings,
customs and immigration.
What to be ready for
and how to be ready for it*

BORDER CROSSINGS

The border: What's to know? You drive up to the man in the booth, he asks where you were born, your citizenship, the purpose of your visit and off you go. Right?

Most of the time it's actually that simple. But not always. Borders are where countries draw the line, and the people charged with overseeing those lines — the customs and immigration officials of the world — either can let you breeze across them or make you toe them, according to their judgment.

While it is up to them whether they let you into their country or not, the traveler's level of preparedness either can facilitate that process or slow it to a crawl. Being well-prepared doesn't guarantee a speedy passage through customs, but it certainly improves your odds.

The main focus of this chapter is customs and immigration and how to get through them as quickly as possible. Rather than duplicate information that's applicable to both outbound and homecoming international travelers, topics such as duty charges, duty-free shops, how and what to declare, and other border-related topics that travelers often are more concerned with on their way home are covered in Chapter 27.

But before we get to that, let's start with an important distinction.

What's the difference between immigration and customs?

One of the best explanations I've ever heard also happens to be the briefest: Immigration is *who* you are; customs is *what* you have with you. So, "Citizenship?" is an immigration question; "What's in your suitcase?" is a customs question.

When you drive to Canada, for example, the customs official in the booth is likely to ask you both types of questions, but that's sort of a preliminary screening. In the event that they want to look deeper into either your background or your luggage, it could be handled by either department (or even both), depending on the line of inquiry.

International travelers generally go through immigration first. Immigration checks your passport and personal identification, and may ask you some background questions. Then, typically, you'll go through customs, where they might search your bag or simply ask what's in it and leave it at that. They also may question you about whether you're carrying any gifts, alcohol, tobacco products, firearms, jewelry, prescription medicine or even contraband.

They'll also want to know if you have anything to declare. In short, have your passport and all other documents ready, be prepared to answer questions and possibly have your luggage searched. Most of the time, it's little more than a formality if you have what you need ready.

What do you need to cross the border?

At the very least, you'll need your passport and personal identification. Immigration often will want you to prove that you have a return ticket and, occasionally, they'll want you to prove that you have enough cash or credit to cover your stay (that you're not indigent or coming into their country to work under the table).

If the country you're traveling to requires a visa to enter, you should be prepared to present it at the border as well. (For more information about visas and who needs them, see Chapter 6.) You'll also be asked if you have anything to declare, and you should have your customs declaration form filled out and ready to present.

What do customs and immigration officials have the right to do?

- When you cross borders, you're legally giving your consent to be questioned or searched by customs and immigration officials.

- They have the right to question you about your citizenship, employment status, your reasons for traveling and pretty much anything else they care to. Do you have to answer them? No. But then, they don't have to let you into their country either.

- They can search your bags and vehicle and conduct personal searches.

- If they find undeclared items with duty owed on them, contraband in your personal possessions or any record of illegal activity in your past, they have the right to detain you, arrest you and impound your vehicle and possessions, depending on the severity of the situation. (Canada won't let anyone who's been arrested for drunk driving in the United States drive across the border into their country.)

Not to worry. Just because customs and immigration have the power to do all those things, that doesn't mean you're automatically going to get the third degree. Most customs and immigration officials are courteous and professional, even genuinely friendly at times. Usually, you're on your way pretty quickly. But they do mean business, and they have a right to ask you about yours. Here are some tips to help you clear customs as quickly as possible.

What (and what not) to do at customs stations

- Be prepared. Keep all of your important documents in order and ready to present to border officials (see checklist).

- Be polite. Remember that you're a guest. When you arrive at the border, you're basically saying, "Let me into your country." They do have a choice.

- Don't get flustered or annoyed. Sometimes border officials will ask you the same question repeatedly to see if you change your answer or appear nervous. Don't get impatient. Just stay calm and courteous and answer their questions.

- Give them honest and complete answers but try not to talk too much. I mention this because sometimes people get nervous at customs and give overly long explanations. You're not expected to provide information that wasn't asked for. If you left out something they want to know, believe me, they'll ask you.

- Take off your sunglasses. Make eye contact, smile and greet the official when you step up to the counter or drive up to the booth. Body language is important. Avoiding eye contact or leaving your sunglasses on sometimes can make officials suspicious of you, which in turn can cause delays.

- If they do ask you to park and go inside or to open your bag or car trunk, don't worry. There are a lot of spot checks and random searches at customs. It doesn't mean you did anything wrong.

- Try to look presentable. Yes, I realize this can be challenging advice to follow if you just got off the plane after an eight-hour overseas flight, but even so, it can make a big difference.

- No jokes. Really, *no jokes.* When they ask if you have anything to declare, you might think you're being really funny by replying with something totally outrageous. They will not even crack a smile, and the next several hours of your life will be a completely humor-free experience.

- Be forthright when declaring goods and have your paperwork ready — receipts, customs declaration form and so on.

- I can't stress this enough: Never *ever* carry anything across an international border for someone you don't know, no matter how harmless or innocent the request may seem.

Additional tips to help you be prepared

- Murphy's law always seems to apply to important documents at customs, which probably is due to the fact that most people are tired and a bit disoriented after international flights. Pre-organization is the best defense. Before you even get off the plane, have your important documents organized and paper-clipped together. (And bring a few extra paper clips with you when you travel.)

- Lightweight, zippered document cases (available from most travel supply retailers) really can come in handy. Most of the time you'll want to keep important documents in your security wallet, but a document case can be very helpful for keeping things organized when you're going through customs and immigration.

- Seasoned travelers often get used to tuning out in-flight announcements, but the flight attendants explain customs procedures for your destination before you arrive. Listen to them. They also hand out customs declaration forms before you land and usually explain the whole procedure over the intercom. Even if you're familiar with the general procedure, it's a good idea to listen to the announcements. They may have information about your specific destination that could be helpful to you.

- This sounds simple, but read and follow the signs when you get off the plane. Even in most foreign countries you'll see signs in English. Most countries divide incoming international travelers into "citizen" and "non-citizen" lines to process them through customs and immigration more efficiently.

Do U.S. citizens need a passport to travel to Canada and Mexico?

- If you are a United States citizen traveling to Canada or Mexico, a passport is not required to enter either country, but unless you're traveling with your birth certificate, you should bring your passport as proof of your citizenship.

- What is required? You must carry proof of your citizenship (birth certificate or government-issued ID) to enter Canada or Mexico, even if you don't have a passport. You may not be asked to produce documented proof of your citizenship, but if they ask and you don't have it, you could be refused entry. If you're smart, you'll obtain a passport.

☑ *Border documents checklist*

No matter what border you're crossing, you need to be able to prove who you are and where you're from. U.S. citizens are required to have documentary proof of their citizenship when returning to the United States. The following forms of identification are acceptable proof of citizenship:

❑ U.S. passport

❑ Naturalization certificate (original)

❑ Your original birth certificate or a certified copy will work when accompanied by a valid (not expired) government-issued photo ID, such as a driver's license.

Note: Voter registration cards no longer are considered proof of citizenship by U.S. Customs.

In addition, you may need:

❑ Government-issued photo ID or driver's license

❑ Customs declaration form

❑ Proof of return ticket

❑ A visa for certain countries

❑ Proof of inoculation (depending on your destination)

❑ If you're driving across the border, you will need your vehicle registration if the vehicle is yours, a signed letter from the owner of the vehicle if the car is borrowed or a copy of the rental contract if it's a rented vehicle. You also will need proof of insurance.

CHAPTER 19

TIPS ABOUT TIPPING

*Where, when, who
and how much to tip*

A GUIDE TO TIPS AND GRATUITIES

The first tip I have about tipping is that any guide is just that: a guide. A ballpark figure. A nice gesture for when the service is good.

Tipping doesn't have to be an all-or-nothing proposition. You can (and should) tip less than 15 percent if the service isn't quite up to snuff; and, naturally, you should feel free to tip more than 15 percent if the service is exceptional. That's your call.

As a general rule, I recommend never feeling pressured to tip more than you feel appropriate. On the other hand, if the service is at least decent, it's not very nice to tip nothing. The following is a general percentage guide for tipping the entire spectrum of service you may encounter out there.

Types of service and appropriate tip percentages
* Rude or genuinely bad: 0 percent
* Flawed but well-meaning: 10 percent
* Good: 15 percent
* Excellent: 20 percent
* Exceptionally conscientious or helpful: 20 percent or more
* Lifesaving: 25 percent or more (it's your call)

Here's a guideline of percentages and amounts for specific services.

At the airport
* Porter or skycap: $1 per bag
* Shoeshine: $2-$5

At the hotel
* Bellman: $1 per bag. Some travelers recommend as much as $2 per bag for the bellman who takes the bags to your room.
* Doorman: $1 for assistance hailing a cab. A tip isn't necessary if the doorman only hails a cab from a cab stand. If the doorman actually hails a cab off the street or calls the cab company for you, a dollar tip is a nice and appropriate thank you. Also, tip $1 per bag for assistance handling your luggage. Some travelers feel 50 cents per bag handled is adequate, except for the bellman who takes bags to your room.
* Hotel maid: $1 per maid for each day of service
* Room service. 15 percent of the bill. If the gratuity is included on the room service bill (and it often is, check before you tip), an additional $1 or more tip for exceptional service is optional but not required.
* Concierge: $5-$10 for special service (making dinner reservations, ordering tickets to a show or a concert).

At the restaurant

- Maitre d': $10 or more if a special service is performed
- Server: 15 percent for good service; 20 percent for excellent service, based on food and beverage costs before tax is added
- Buffet attendant or server: $1 from each person in your group
- Bartender or cocktail server: $1-$2 for each round of drinks or 15 percent of the total check amount; 20 percent for excellent service
- Coat check: $1 per coat; $2 if you check a coat and a hat

Drivers and others

- Taxi drivers: $1-$5 according to the length of the trip and the quality of the service
- Limo drivers: 15 percent for good service; 20 percent for excellent service
- Bus tours: $1 per person for the tour guide and the driver. If you're traveling by yourself, $2 is a decent tip for a one- to two-hour tour.
- Valet parking attendant: $5-$10 as you enter and leave the establishment (often signs are posted with expected amounts, look for them)

Miscellaneous

- Spa personnel: 15 percent for good service; 20 percent for excellent service
- Hair stylist: 15 percent for good service; 20 percent for excellent service
- Bathroom attendant: $1. Note: In Europe, many restrooms have an attendant, and to use the facilities you have to tip a nominal amount.

An assortment of tipping tips, strategies and tactics

- Always budget your tip money ahead of time. Put tip money aside at the beginning (preferably in an envelope) of the trip.
- Get a little, business card-size tip rate table to help you calculate tips accurately. These are quick reference guides that fit neatly in your wallet.
- Bring small denominations of the local currency with you wherever you go. It's preferable not to have to ask for change when you're tipping.
- Take extra envelopes to put tip money in. Also, people love a personal note of thanks, whether it's written on the envelope or on a thank you card inside the envelope.
- Remember, even if you don't have any of the local currency handy, a U.S. $1 bill is a universally acceptable tip almost anywhere in the world.
- If you're giving someone a particularly nice tip, hand delivering it is the best way to go for two reasons. One, a personal thanks is a nice touch that's almost always appreciated. Two, it guarantees that the tip ends up in the hands of the person for whom it was intended.

- Read the bottom of the bill to see if the gratuity already has been included. In many parts of the world, a 15 percent gratuity automatically is added to café and restaurant bills. This is a standard practice in France, for example. Look for the words *service compris*. Translating loosely from French, that means "you don't have to leave additional money on the table unless the service was really incredible."
- Tipping etiquette varies dramatically around the world, and it's not a universally practiced custom. In China, Russia and many parts of Africa, it's actively discouraged. Know before you go. A good destination-specific guidebook should have that information.
- Never tip uniformed personnel, such as a policeman, a ship's officer, security personnel, military personnel or a customs agent. They don't call that tipping. They call it bribery — whether you meant it that way or not.

Where the expression 'tip' comes from

I always thought the expression "tip" came from getting a "tip of the hat" for putting a coin in a doorman's hand or something along those lines. According to my parents, it's an acronym that means "to insure promptness."

Here are some techniques that help ensure prompt service:

- If you're going on a cruise, many travelers wisely tip half their budgeted tip money for the staff up front and give out the rest later.
- In crowded bars, a larger tip for the first drink or round of drinks, often can ensure more attentive service from a cocktail server or bartender.
- Here's a tipping custom I really like, most commonly exercised in England, Scotland, Ireland and Australia: When paying for a round of drinks, put in enough extra money to pay for one more full-price drink. As you turn the money over to the bartender, say. "And one for yourself." It's a nice way of saying, "Thanks for the good service and have one on me." It's also understood that you don't expect any change back and that the bartender is free to keep the tip in monetary form or convert it to liquid assets.
- It's not customary to tip hotel housekeeping for a one-night stay, but I recommend leaving a nice tip in an envelope the morning after the first night of a multiple-night stay.

Many people weren't raised to consider tipping, beyond leaving the server a tip. In many ways, tipping is a vestige of a more genteel era of travel. But I think knowing how to approach tipping with confidence and fairness is an important skill for modern world travelers.

CHAPTER 20

AT THE HOTEL

*Staying the night at your
destination accommodations*

ARRIVAL

Ahhhh. You made it. Home sweet home away from home at last: the hotel. Everything in its right place. Hopefully. Hotels can be a traveler's sanctuary or a pain in the neck — depending on the quality of the management, the plumbing and the mattress.

On a good day (or night), they'll exceed your best expectations and win your loyalty. Other times, they'll disappoint you — and it helps to know what your options are when and if that happens.

There also are some finer points of safety, security, comfort and a few tips about hotel service that any hotel guest should know about. We'll get to those topics in a moment.

EXPECTATIONS AT THE HOTEL

First things first: When you arrive, check out your room. Do the accommodations match what you were promised when you made the reservation? If not, go back to the front desk and speak with the desk clerk or the manager on duty if necessary. Let them know what or where the problem is and give them a chance to fix it.

The reason you always want to get your hotel reservations in writing (whether they're faxed, mailed or e-mailed to you from the hotel management at your request) is that it gives you more leverage — and the hotel less wiggle room — if for any reason they mess up your reservation.

By the time you arrive at the hotel you're usually tired and just want to settle in for the night, and there may not even be alternate accommodations readily available even if you want them. That's not exactly the best position to negotiate from if things aren't right. Having your reservations in writing can help you get what you were promised or get you compensated for promises not delivered.

TIPS ABOUT HOTEL SAFETY, SECURITY, COMFORT AND SERVICE

Most hotel stays do, in fact, go more or less according to plan without any unfortunate problems. However, there are some things travelers should know and do to increase their odds of having a good stay — or to deal with problems effectively if they do arise.

Here are some ways to improve your safety, security and comfort, along with information about hotel personnel and service you might need to know. As always, safety first.

Check-in checklist — does your room check out?

 The following checklist provides some guidelines for determining if your room is up to snuff. I understand there are circumstances under which travelers have to settle for less than the ideal — even if only for a night. I also realize that many European hotel rooms don't have their own TV or phone.

These items are on the list to check when and where it's appropriate:

1. Is the room clean?
2. Is the bedding laundered and fresh?
3. Is the bathroom (shared or private) clean?
4. Are the towels clean?
5. Is there adequate water pressure?

6. Does the phone work?
7. Are all the door and window locks in good working order?
8. Is the room secure?
9. Is it quiet enough?
10. Does the TV work?

Safety tips

Hotel safety boils down to two primary issues: personal security and fire safety. First, check out the U.S. Fire Administration website at usfa.fema.gov. It's filled with potentially lifesaving information, with an entire section of the site devoted to hotel fire safety. In the meantime, here are some fire safety tips you'll want to check out before you check in.

Plan ahead

• When making your reservations, ask if the hotel or motel has smoke detectors and fire sprinklers.

• When you travel, take a flashlight with you and bring it to your hotel room.

• Read your hotel's fire evacuation plan carefully. If one isn't posted in your room, request one from the front desk.

• Locate the two exits nearest your room.

• Count the number of doors between your room and the exits. This will help you exit more quickly in the event of an emergency evacuation.

- Locate the fire alarms on your floor.
- Never smoke in bed.
- Consider bringing a travel smoke alarm. These are available at most travel supply stores.
- If you're traveling with kids, make sure they know what to do in an emergency, too.

Security tips

- Be aware of the people around you when you check in. If you feel that someone is deliberately eavesdropping on your conversation in order to hear your room number, discreetly ask the desk clerk if you can switch rooms.
- Verify while making reservations that the hotel's rooms have deadbolts and peepholes.
- Watch out for anyone who offers to carry your bags who obviously isn't a member of the hotel staff.
- If you think someone is following you to your room, return to the front desk and ask for a member of the staff or hotel security to escort you to your room.
- Never leave your key out in the open, such as on the table at the restaurant or bar, or on a towel or patio table poolside. Always guard your room key carefully.
- Always use the deadbolt lock and supplementary locking devices. Make sure windows and the patio or balcony doors are securely locked, too. Whenever you enter or exit your hotel room, make sure the door is securely shut and locked — even if you only plan to be gone a minute or two.
- Never leave valuables in your hotel room. Store valuables in the hotel safe.
- Never open the door to anyone you don't know — unless you ordered room service. Even so, check the peephole to verify who they are.
- Have any deliveries other than room service brought to the front desk.
- If someone at the door claims to be from hotel maintenance or engineering, call the front desk to verify.
- Consider purchasing a portable door alarm (available at most travel supply stores).
- Try to get a room on the second floor or higher.

Easy luxuries and inexpensive comforts to make your stay more enjoyable

Sometimes a hotel room is just a place to sleep. But sometimes it's a refuge from the world — especially if you're 5,000 miles from home in some place you've never been before, dealing with culture shock, homesickness or simply being tired.

There are times when four walls, a bed and access to hot water are the only things you want. Refuge and comfort. Hot bath. Comfortable sweats. A good book to read while propped up in bed using all the pillows.

Here are some low-budget ways to turn your room into a mini-spa and give yourself a break:

- Put a bouquet of flowers in your hotel room to cheer things up. I don't necessarily mean you should run to the nearest florist shop and drop $50 on a bouquet. Many places in the world have beautiful open-air markets and farmer's markets with local vendors who sell fresh-cut flowers for reasonable prices. This isn't just some frilly, feel-good tip, but so what if it were? Flowers are the original air freshener — the very thing people always are trying to make air fresheners (and rooms) smell like. And they bring color and cheer to a room. Support your local grower, as they say at the farmer's market. You always can use the ice bucket for a vase in a pinch.
- Bring your own pair of slippers with you. Slippers generally are very light and packable, and they can add a lot of comfort. (Or bring sockettes.)
- Bring a bathrobe. Note: I admit that bathrobes aren't that packable. Sometimes you have to use a trade-out system, leaving certain items behind in order to have room for a particular comfort you can't live without. For some travelers, that item is their own pillow. You decide what's essential for you.
- Some hotels provide robes. Don't be shy about using them.
- A travel candle can be very relaxing for a candlelit bath. Just be careful not to set anything on fire or fall asleep with a candle burning.
- Bring travel-size bath salts or bubble bath with you. They're perfect for a hot soak after a long day of walking and sightseeing.
- Bring herbal tea.

- If you're staying with others, let them know where you're going and when they can expect you back if you go off on your own.
- Use the main entrance to the hotel after nightfall.
- Consider using valet parking.
- Don't use the "service wanted" door tag. It lets thieves know the room is empty.
- Report any disturbances in the hall or outside on the street to the front desk.
- Close the curtains — especially at night and when you leave your room — if anyone can see through the window from outside your room.
- If you're staying in a hotel, bed-and-breakfast or hostel with a shared bath down the hall, always take your key and your security wallet with you and keep them in sight when you bathe. And remember to lock both your room and the bathroom door.

Comfort tips

When it comes to hotel comforts, it's not just a matter of what you find when you arrive. It's knowing how to bring comforts with you and how to create them out of the resources available to you. Here are some ideas:

- The all-purpose comfort and sleep combo of earplugs and an eye mask can help you sleep without being disturbed by noise or light. Standard warning: Use these items at your own discretion. Don't let them compromise your security.
- I also recommend bringing a small night light with you when you travel. Unfamiliar rooms can be disorienting in the dark. This is a small item that can make a big difference.
- Remember: If you want more pillows, blankets or towels, you always can call the front desk and have housekeeping send them up.
- Bring duct tape (wrapped around a pencil) or extra safety pins to keep room curtains closed — especially if you need to sleep during the day.
- A lot of hotel air systems seem to have two settings: too hot or too cold, but there usually is a fresh-air setting if you need a break from the heat or the cold. Turning on the bathroom fan and leaving the bathroom door open also can be a good way to air out your room.
- Pull the bedspread off the bed and stow it away in the closet. Hotel bedspreads are washed very infrequently.

- Many travelers will not risk less-than-sanitary bedding and prefer to unroll a sleeping bag on top of the bed or use a sleep sack. Sleep sacks are inexpensive, lightweight, packable sacks you can slip into. A silk sleep sack can add a bit of warmth or be the perfect bedding for hot, humid destinations. It provides a layer between you and hotel bedding.

- Leggings or sweats make good jammies and lounging-around wear. (They're also a practical and modest solution for lodgings with shared bathrooms such as some bed-and-breakfasts, many European hotels and most hostels.)

- Most hotel rooms seem to come with a little four-cup coffeepot and a couple of filter pouches of regular and decaf coffee. If you like strong coffee, try this trick: Use one pouch of regular and one of decaf to make just one pot. You get a good, strong pot of coffee without doubling your caffeine intake.

- If you're one of the many travelers in the world who really has to have good coffee in the morning, I recommend bringing at least a small supply of your favorite coffee with you. And what if the hotel room doesn't have a coffeepot? The best, sure-fire portable system I know of is the mini French press. Made out of plastic, it is light, compact and holds about two cups. Store it in a resealable plastic bag.

- Bring your own sweetener for your tea or your coffee if you like a particular brand.

- Room service is never inexpensive, but it can be a godsend when you've finally found the hotel, settled into your room and just don't want to go out again — much less find something to eat in an unfamiliar city at night.

OF CHARGES AND CHECKOUTS: WHAT'S THE REAL BOTTOM LINE?

Why is it that the final bill is higher — and occasionally even *much* higher — than the price you were quoted when you made the reservation? Generally, it's a combination of factors, hidden charges you didn't even know to look for or ask about beforehand. Here's a checklist of the usual culprits.

Hotel taxes

When you make reservations within the United States, be certain to ask how much tax is included. You might think it's the standard sales tax for whichever state you're staying in. Wrong. One way that municipalities raise taxes and build things such as football stadiums without

Hotel staffing and protocols

Job descriptions and duties: the hotel staff. It's certainly no disgrace not to know what, exactly, it is that a concierge does for a living. A lot of us were raised on family road trips, staying at the Holiday Inn with our parents and siblings. In those days, the burning question was, "Do they have a pool?" not, "What should we tip the concierge for getting us dinner reservations at the top of the Space Needle at 7 p.m.?"

But in many parts of the world, the old school, Old World hierarchy of hotel staffing and protocols still is firmly in place. Here's a quick guide to who does what. You'll find some of these functions only at more upscale properties.

Bellman. Some bellmen only work in the lobby, assisting guests with their bags between the door and the front desk. Other bellmen assist guests with their bags from the front desk to the room.

Doorman. This is the person who mans the front door of the hotel: opening the door, assisting guests with their bags from the curb to the door (and vice versa), and calling and hailing cabs for guests.

Concierge. *Concierge* is a French word that literally means the person who's in charge of the entrance of a building, sometimes known as the front desk manager. He or she also can help with things such as ordering a cab, making dinner or show reservations.

Housecleaning/maid. These are the people who clean your room and replace the towels and bedding — not to be confused with room service.

Room service. Not to be confused with housekeeping, room service means meal and beverage delivery to your room from the hotel restaurant. Not all hotels have room service, and none of them seems to have inexpensive room service. But it can be very convenient and a nice indulgence.

Maitre d'. Maitre d' is short for *maitre d'hôtel*, which means the headwaiter at the hotel restaurant. The maitre d' oversees the wait staff and, in most cases, handles the dinner reservations.

provoking the locals is to selectively raise the sales tax on things like guest services: rental cars and hotel rooms.

In many U.S. cities, the tax percentage is as high as 15 percent. In Europe, it gets even steeper, with VAT (value-added tax) as high as 30 percent. There's no way around it, so the best thing you can do is to find out how much it'll cost you and budget it into your trip.

Room service charges

If you do get room service, check the bill carefully — especially before you tip. In many hotels, the gratuity automatically is added on (read the fine print at the bottom), and it's usually 15 percent to 18 percent. If you didn't know that when you put room service on your room tab, it can be a bit of a shocker when you get the final bill.

Phone charges

If you've ever tried to decipher so-called disclosure cards (the plastic cards next to the phone in most hotel rooms that allegedly explain how the charges work), you know they sometimes can be about as easy to understand as a genetic engineering manual written in Latin.

The bottom line is that a lot of hotels charge outrageous amounts of money for you to use the phone in your room. "No problem," you think. "I'll use my calling card." It should be so easy. Many hotels won't let you access toll-free numbers from your room phone. Or they'll actually channel your toll-free call to their own long-distance carrier, and you still get stuck with a big bill.

One way to beat this system is to use a cell phone if you've got one with you. You also can go to the pay phone in the lobby and use your calling card number from there at the usual rate.

Delivery charges

If you receive a fax, a message, mail or a package, and the hotel staff offers to deliver it to your room, you'd be better off picking it up at the front desk instead. Many hotels actually will tack on a delivery charge even if they just bring a piece of paper to your room, although they don't necessarily tell you that. You just find out when you get the bill.

Minibar charges

That cute little fridge in your room with goodies in it? It's not an amenity. Wait until you see what they charge you for that soda. The minibar is one of the worst values for your travel dollar imaginable.

How does it work? They stock it, take inventory on the contents and charge you top dollar (as much as $6 for a soda) for anything you consume. It's much better to bring some goodies with you if you want to settle into your room for the night and think you might get hungry or thirsty.

And the moral is . . .

Before you check out, check out the charges on your bill. Ask for an explanation of any charges or add-ons that aren't clear. Dispute any charges that can't be explained to your satisfaction. For more information about ways to deal with grievances and discrepancies, see Chapter 25.

Bring the right information

When you check in to a hotel or motel:

1. Have your written confirmation available and identify yourself as a AAA member by showing your membership card.

2. You are entitled to a clean and comfortable environment.

3. You should question any additional charges for the room or other unauthorized charges.

4. If your room or stay is not satisfactory, you should immediately address the problem with management and expect an acceptable resolution.

5. You are entitled to an itemized receipt when you check out.

Pat Szejh Tichonoff
AAA Member Relations
Heathrow, Fla.

CHAPTER 21

FOREIGN CORRESPONDENCE

*Staying in touch
and how to go about it*

BRAVE NEW CONNECTED WORLD

The world is a complicated place, but it has never been easier to keep in touch — especially for travelers. These days, you can log on in Copenhagen, make an online reservation for a hotel room in Barcelona the following week and e-mail your mom in Michigan before the cyber-cafe proprietor even has a chance to bring you the bottle of juice and the croissant you ordered.

The details behind Internet technology and cellular communications can be mind-boggling, but harnessing this technology for your own benefit is not really that difficult. For the overseas traveler, e-mail is a much cheaper way to keep in touch than using pay phones or cell phones. And in most cases, it's easier and more convenient than dealing with foreign postal systems.

Phones around the world

Using the phone usually is a simple matter when you're traveling in North America, whether it's a calling card call placed on a pay phone or a personal cell phone. But when you go overseas, things get more complicated.

The first decision you have to make is whether or not you really need to have a cell phone with you. The advantage is all of the advantages you'd have with a cell phone anywhere. The disadvantage is the cost — which can be prohibitive for travelers on a budget — and the risk of loss or theft.

Cell phone considerations

But let's say you want to bring a cell phone. If you already have one, contact your service provider and find out whether your particular phone will work overseas. North American cell phones operate on a different frequency than their European counterparts.

If you're traveling overseas, you'll need a "dual-band" phone or, even better, a "tri-band" phone — both of which are available in the United States. If you don't have a dual-band or tri-band phone, they aren't hard to come by. Often you can rent or buy one from your current provider and move your existing account temporarily to that phone.

The coverage you'll need

You'll not only need the right cell phone, but you'll need global coverage in order to use it. And it doesn't come cheap. However, you can get global access for specific periods of time from any number of service providers.

Don't be intimidated

You would need a master's degree from MIT to thoroughly understand the ins and outs of modern global telecommunications. Don't bother. You're a consumer; telecommunications companies want to sell you these services.

Make them answer your questions and give you a price. Then decide if they have the service you need and whether or not it's worth it. Whether or not you already have a cell phone, it's a good idea to comparison shop.

Questions to ask your cell phone service provider

The best place to start gathering information and pricing things out is with your own cell phone service provider, if you have one. Here are the main things you'll need to know:

- Will your current handset work at your specific destination?

- If not, do they have a program where you can rent one that will?

- Do they have global coverage?

- If so, do they have a short-term global coverage program for travelers?

- Ask for details about different calling rates for different time zones. Is there a time of day or days of the week that will be cheaper to call from your destination?

- Get the specifics of their global coverage. Roaming charges can be very expensive if coverage is spotty. If you're paying for global coverage, make sure it covers your particular destinations.

- Finally, what's all of it going to cost you (phone, global coverage, long-distance rates)?

Pay phones and phone cards

Public telephones in other countries can be a bit of a trial. We'll have to discuss this topic in somewhat general terms because every country has its own pay phone system, and there's no international standard to speak of. Here are some tips for using pay phones abroad:

- Wherever you go, either find out how the pay phones work before you get there or at least get a general idea as soon as possible after you arrive.

- One important thing to know is foreign pay phones that take money don't always take it at one time. Before you put money in a foreign pay phone only to discover you put it in at the wrong time and lost it, find out what the standard is for that particular country.

- If you need assistance, most foreign phone books have a front section in English, often with instructions about how to contact an English-speaking operator.

- To use a pay phone in most foreign countries, you need a calling card from the country you're in. Country-specific calling cards generally can be found at post offices, train stations, in many shops and at National Tourist Offices. If the National Tourist Office doesn't sell them, they'll be able to tell you where to find them. Country-specific calling cards generally have a microchip or magnetic strip, and they're based on stored credits. You buy a card that's worth a certain number of credits, and you can see how many credits you have left on a little screen when you use the pay phone. Needless to say, long-distance calls eat up credits at a much faster rate.

- Don't use country-specific calling cards to make long-distance calls home. This is never a good deal. Obtain an international calling card from your long-distance carrier *before* you leave home. They work pretty much the same as a regular calling card works at home. Each long-distance company has its own international access numbers for each country it services. Here's the drill: You use your country-specific calling card just to access the pay phone, then you place your long-distance call using the international calling card you got from your own long-distance carrier. The bill shows up on your phone bill at home. This way, you don't eat up all the credits on your country-specific calling card because you're not using it to place a long-distance call. You're only using it to gain access to the pay phone.

You want cash and you want it now

 To know where the closest ATMs are to your hotel, check out Visa and MaterCard's ATM locater websites before you travel. You can search through their worldwide database before you begin your trip. Their addresses are usa.visa.com and mastercard.com.

Melody Bruner
AAA Travel Professional
Topeka, Kan.

- You don't *always* have to use your country-specific calling card to place a call using your international long-distance card. Sometimes you can just pick up the pay phone receiver, dial the necessary numbers shown on your international phone card and bypass using the country-specific calling card altogether. Strangely enough, this not only varies from country to country, but from *pay phone* to *pay phone* in any given country.

- If for any reason you have trouble using either your country-specific calling card or your international calling card, don't automatically assume the card is at fault. Foreign pay phones and phone systems can be erratic. If you have a problem or can't get through, *always try another pay phone.* If, for instance, you're at the train station where there's a bank of pay phones and you have trouble with more than one phone, walk 50 feet to a different bank of phones and try one of them before you assume your calling card is at fault. I prefer to buy and use phone cards or calling cards with a pre-purchased number of minutes. A beep tells you when you have one minute left. I buy them in each country and if I don't use the time, then I give it to a student I meet on the train. Or even better, buy one you can use in several countries.

Package deals for phone and Internet service

Here's an interesting development you'll want to know about: A number of telecommunications companies are offering package deals on international phone service and Internet access. These package deals provide an international calling card, voice mail you can pick up either by phone or online, a free e-mail account, secure online storage for important travel and personal information (passport number, reservation info), and "rechargeable cards" — meaning you can phone the provider or go online and get more time on your prepaid international calling card by charging it on a credit card.

I predict these multipurpose package programs will be an increasingly popular solution for travelers who want to maximize their options for staying in touch with a minimum amount of hassle.

Getting online overseas

Whether you're booking reservations online, trying to find lodgings in the next city you'll be visiting or looking up the latest train schedule, the nearly instant access to information that the Internet provides makes it a tremendous resource for travelers on the road. And it's not hard to connect, even if you don't have a laptop with you.

Staying in touch via e-mail

E-mail offers travelers a number of benefits. For one thing, it's a lot cheaper than long-distance calling and much faster than snail mail. All you need to do is to set up an account with an Internet service provider.

Both Yahoo! Mail (yahoo.com) and Hotmail (hotmail.com) offer free e-mail accounts that you can set up online, and you'll be able to send and receive e-mails from any place in the world where you can get access to the World Wide Web.

How do you get access?

Cybercafes

Cybercafes have sprung up all over the world in the last several years, and you even can find them on cruise ships these days. They're particularly popular in Europe where access to the Internet is available in thousands of cafes, coffee shops and even Laundromats.

Some cybercafes charge you only for the time you're logged on; some charge in blocks of an hour. Usually, it's very affordable, sometimes as low as $2 an hour with a good exchange rate, but in general around $5-$10 an hour. All you need to keep in touch via e-mail is your own account and a few spare minutes in a cybercafe.

Online resources to help you find cybercafes

The thing about cybercafes is that they have a tendency to appear and disappear, so information about where to find them tends to be more accurate and up-to-date online than it is in print. Check out these two sites for starters:

Easyeverything.com — This is the home site for Easy Internet Cafe, a chain of cybercafes in Europe and the United States. Easy Internet Cafe took the home-grown cottage industry of cybercafes and created a chain (look for the big orange signs) of cybercafes with up-to-date equipment and services (broadband access, for example) and reasonable prices. Their website will tell you where you can find their cafes throughout the world.

Netcafes.com — Another great spot to locate cybercafes around the world, netcafes.com has more than 4,000 listings for cybercafes in 148 countries. Netcafes.com is a user-friendly site where it's simple to search for cafes by city or country.

Bringing your own computer

Most laptops — and certainly the cheap ones — are pretty fragile when it comes to the kind of knocks world travel can dish out. For a lot of them, it's *game over* if they're dropped on a hard surface even once.

Until recently, the dilemma has been that the sturdy ones are too heavy to lug around the world, and the light ones are too delicate. However, there's been an encouraging trend toward laptops that are both light and resilient — but they don't come cheap. You should also consider a padded computer sleeve, which is available at luggage and travel stores.

My advice is this: If you really *need* a laptop computer, bring one with you. But either bring a cheap one that won't break your heart if you break its hard drive, or take the plunge and get a good one that can take the punishment. Otherwise, use cybercafes.

There's really no need to schlep a laptop around the world if you only want it for e-mail or Internet access. Even if you have a good laptop, cybercafes can be a lot more convenient because everything's already connected and ready to go.

Save a buck or two

When traveling internationally, be sure to fully understand charges on international phone calls. Many times, the least expensive way to call from a destination such as Mexico is to call collect. And be aware that prepaid phone calls that are valid in the United States will not necessarily work when calling from your international destination, even though they say that they will.

Crystal Dittman
AAA Travel Professional
Topeka, Kan.

Snail mail

Whatever difficulties it may have (and it has had to contend with some *doozies),* the U.S. Postal Service is a miracle of efficiency and professionalism compared to 99 percent of the postal systems in the rest of the world. I am not being even *slightly* sarcastic here. Once you've experienced other countries' postal services, you'll want to buy your mail carrier back home flowers and chocolates.

This doesn't mean they're all bad. They're not. But few of them stack up to the consistent quality of service found in the United States. The quality of post offices can range dramatically not only from country to country but from post office to post office *within* a country.

However, if you want to keep in touch using conventional mail when you travel overseas, you'll have to deal with the post office. The majority of travelers usually only want one of two things in a foreign post office (postcard stamps or airmail letters), and that's not too difficult to manage.

Here are some tips for sending and receiving mail abroad:

• Learn the words for "postcard," "stamp" and "airmail letter." A few words can go a long way. Look for phrase books with location-specific words and phrases.

• If you just need to buy postcard stamps, you can show the postal clerk your stack of unstamped postcards and point to the empty stamp boxes on the cards.

• For anyone who may not have seen them before, airmail letters (sometimes known as *aerograms)* are those nifty blue sheets of pre-gummed, pre-stamped paper that you can write a letter on, then fold up and seal like an envelope. They're the easiest way to send a letter from Europe.

• Sending packages home is a trickier proposition — especially if you don't speak the language and you're trying to do something like insure the contents. In many cases, you're better off using a private international carrier (such as FedEx) with computerized delivery tracking, which lets you check your package's progress online. Check out different private carriers' websites for prices and availability of overseas service. The main advantage of using systems such as FedEx is that you avoid variable postal systems.

• If you're using American Express® Traveler's Cheques or you have an American Express credit card, you can have mail sent to you anywhere they have American Express offices.

- You also can receive mail care of general delivery at a city's main post office. The standard policy is to hold your mail for up to 30 days, after which it gets returned to the sender. You'll be required to show your passport when you come in to pick up your mail.
- Hours of operation can be erratic in foreign post offices. Never assume you'll be able to use the post office between noon and 3 p.m., as the midday break is a very flexible concept in many parts of the world. Generally, you're better off conducting any post office business in the morning.

National Tourist Offices are a great resource when you have questions about a particular country's postal system (including where to find the post office), where to find cybercafes and how the phone system works.

When in doubt, go to the National Tourist Office and ask them, "What's the best way to do this?" In many countries, you can buy the phone card you'll need to work their pay phones from the National Tourist Office.

One last piece of advice

When you start asking about Internet access, phone cards, cell phones and global coverage, people often will try to sell you stuff right away. Don't be afraid to ask all the questions you need to, but don't commit to purchasing anything until you're ready.

Find out what your options are, get the information you need and don't make a purchase until you know it's the right decision for you. This is one reason I suggest seeking out information at National Tourist Offices. Generally, they're more concerned with providing you information than selling you something.

CHAPTER 22

SECURITY STRATEGIES

*Keeping your head,
thinking on your feet,
looking and being streetwise*

SECURITY STRATEGIES AND PROCEDURES

Throughout this book, you'll find all sorts of security tips, by topic, in nearly every chapter. There's a lot to know. You start writing security tips, and inevitably you end up thinking, "What did I miss?"

Every situation is case-specific, but the underlying truth about security is always the same: Travelers don't want to find themselves in a situation where they're at a distinct disadvantage and a long way from home. That's a lousy combination and a good scenario to avoid.

No matter how careful you are, security is never guaranteed. But there are a lot of things travelers can do to keep themselves out of harm's way. Specific tips can be a big help. For example, always use a security wallet when you travel.

But beneath the surface of every tip there usually is an underlying security strategy that can be applied to all sorts of different situations and destinations. In this chapter, we'll take a look at what you might call standard operational security procedures.

Hold on to those smaller hands

When visiting theme parks, zoos or traveling through busy airports, wear a fanny pack with tickets, money, small snacks and other items. Then you don't have to let go of your children's little hands. (They always seem to wander off at busy places.)

AAA Travel Consultant
Bluffton, S.C.

STRATEGY

Look like you know where you're going even when you don't

This is a useful traveler's skill, especially in unfamiliar cities. Occasionally, you get lost or turned around for a few minutes. It happens. It's how you react that matters.

Even if you're disoriented, it helps not to look like you are. People who prey on tourists and travelers tend to start with the ones who look helpless or confused. So you need to have what I call your "traveler's game face." This would be a look of calm, purpose and determination that you can put on even when you're not necessarily feeling that way.

If you do get lost, the best thing to do is to either walk with purpose like you know where you're going until you find your way or simply stop and figure it out.

I personally like smaller, portable guidebooks that have lots of good maps in them. You can sit on the subway or in a cafe and figure out exactly where you are, and you just look like you're sitting there reading a paperback. Standing in the middle of the sidewalk fussing with a big folding map with a worried look on your face is like hanging out a sign that says, "I'm lost. I'm not from here. Please take advantage of me." Not a good idea. Asking directions from the locals is a perfectly good way to get your bearings again. But sometimes it takes awhile to find the right person to ask. In the meantime, try not to *look* lost.

Out of sight, out of mind

Here's one of the great principles of theft prevention: Out of sight, out of mind. In other words, most thieves don't like to work on speculation because there's too much risk involved. They'd much rather break out a car window to grab a bag they can see is sitting right there on the seat than break into the trunk of a car in the hope that there *might* be something worth stealing in there.

This "out of sight, out of mind" principle is one reason security wallets are so effective. Thieves know people use them, but they can't be

Packing your day bag

The way you pack your day bag can increase your personal security. As a rule, it's a good idea not to advertise the fact that you're wearing a security wallet. Here's a practical way to do that: Keep $75 to $100 cash in small denominations of the local currency easily accessible.

There are two advantages to this system: You can make small purchases without advertising you're wearing a security wallet and, worst-case scenario, if your day bag is lost or stolen, you're out only $75-$100 in cash and maybe your camera, sunglasses, sunscreen and a guidebook or two, which might be inconvenient, but it wouldn't be devastating.

Meanwhile, your passport, your ID, your train pass and your credit cards are all still safely tucked away in your security wallet.

sure you're wearing one. That's why most thieves prefer to pick on the guy who wears a big wallet in his back pocket or the tourist who leaves her purse sitting on the chair next to her at the outdoor cafe.

Be vigilant

Be aware of your surroundings and the people in them. Vigilance doesn't mean being reflexively afraid or paranoid. It means calmly, alertly keeping at least one eye on what's going on around you and your luggage, especially in crowded places such as airports, train stations and subways.

Thieves like airports and train stations because there are lots of opportunities, as well as lots of noise and commotion. It's easy to be anonymous and blend into the crowd, and airports and tourist attractions are full of people who are distracted and on unfamiliar ground.

Crowded trains, markets and public events always are an opportunity for pickpockets and other unsavory people to try and take advantage of the unaware. An ounce of vigilance is worth a ton of regret. Watch your bag. Take precautions. Thieves generally prefer to avoid common-sense travelers who are on their guard.

Travel light

Traveling light not only is more convenient, it makes security easier. If you have one personal bag you can sling over your shoulder and keep in front of you and one piece of carry on-size wheeled luggage, it's much easier to keep an eye on your luggage, and you're extremely mobile if and when you need to be. You've only got two hands, so it's hard to hold onto more than two pieces of luggage.

Trust your gut instinct

Learn to trust your instincts as a traveler. Maybe there isn't a "logical" reason why you don't want to get into the elevator alone. So don't get on the elevator. Logic and good manners are necessary things to have when you're a world traveler, but try not to let them undermine your gut instinct.

Dealing with panhandlers

Unless you have your own personal Lear jet, limousine service and security detail, you will encounter poor people when you travel: the genuinely hungry, homeless and often harmless people. You'll also find hucksters, hustlers and hassles on the streets of nearly every city of any country in the world. From Atlanta to San Francisco. From Hong Kong to Guatemala City, it's commonplace to see poverty in its cruelest form: desperate children.

Be careful, be careful, be careful

1. Especially be watchful of your cash, credit cards and traveler's checks. When retrieving money from your wallet or purse, be an inconspicuous as possible.
2. Wear a minimal amount of jewelry. Leave your best pieces at home.
3. Don't wear bright, loud or tourist-type clothes that draw attention to you.
4. Travel in pairs.
5. Arrange for taxicabs with a hotel employee. Negotiate the rate before you depart. Arrange for the same cab driver to pick you up and return you to the hotel.
6. Carry the hotel's matchpacks so that if you get lost, you can ask people to direct you to the hotel.
7. Being on vacation doesn't mean you should let your guard down. Have fun and enjoy yourself, but always be aware of your surroundings!

AAA General Manager
Hendersonville Service Office
Hendersonville, N.C.

No travel guide can tell you how and when to act on your conscience. That's your business, your judgment call. The main issue with panhandlers when you travel is personal safety. Being stopped by a panhandler can put you in a vulnerable position — especially if you open your purse, bag or money belt to hand them some cash.

And there are many places in the world where handing a begging child a coin is an irresistible urge that can be an invitation to be mobbed by dozens of children. It's always best to be vigilant if someone you don't know tries to stall you for any reason.

ONE FINAL THOUGHT

Everybody's heard cautionary tales. Let them be just that: cautionary tales that keep you on your guard. But don't let them ruin your trip.

For the most part, the worst-case scenario doesn't happen. Security means being as prepared as you can be — it doesn't mean being nervous all the time. Be safe and be vigilant, but don't forget to have fun. That's why you went on vacation to begin with, right?

CHAPTER 23

WOMEN TRAVELING ALONE

*Collected tips
and considerations*

TIP 1
Be prepared and use common sense

Writing safety tips for women who travel alone requires a delicate balance. On the one hand, I want to present a realistic view of the types of behavior you may encounter and the precautions you need to take to ensure your personal safety.

On the other hand, I don't want to discourage any woman from traveling on her own. I love to travel solo, and I encourage women who want to see the world by themselves to get out and do it. I assure you, that's the spirit in which these tips were written. They're meant to prevent trouble, not travel.

You should approach traveling alone the same way you would approach defensive driving. Being a good defensive driver doesn't mean being afraid to drive the car because of all the things that *might* go wrong. It means knowing the risks, anticipating potential hazards in order to avoid them and having a plan of action if something should go wrong.

Whether they realize it or not, most women already have many of the skills they need to be safe travelers just by virtue of having grown up, worked and lived in their own hometowns. The difference is at home we know the lay of the land, the cultural assumptions (for good or bad) and what to expect from the locals. That's what's known as the *home-team advantage*, and there are some ways to have it even when you're not actually on your own home court.

PLANNING AHEAD

- Knowledge is indeed power, and the more knowledge you have about your destination before you get there, the better. Know what to expect before you arrive. Do your homework, read a guidebook, be familiar with the local customs and mores. You'll want to have at least a basic understanding of women's social status in the country you're traveling to. And you'll need to know how the locals view unaccompanied female travelers.

- If you're traveling alone for the first time, I suggest starting with a destination where women's social status is comparable to what you're used to at home. If you've never traveled by yourself before, you probably don't want to start in places such as Turkey, India or Egypt.

- If you do choose to travel off the beaten path, try to talk with someone who's been there. Reap the benefit of their personal experience — especially a woman's experience. A male friend may be able to tell you about some great sights or local delicacies you wouldn't want to miss, but he won't necessarily be able to provide much insight about what it will be like for you as a woman alone.

• The previous tip also applies to destinations that *aren't* off the beaten path. Even if you're considering a more conventional or popular destination, seek out the solo woman traveler who's been there and ask her questions. A male friend's perspective on how wonderful it is to travel alone through Italy by train may well be completely different from what a female friend would tell you about the exact same trip.

• Know the lay of the land before you get there. If you're staying in the city, study maps and guidebooks before you go. Have a handy, portable map with you. A small travel compass also can be a very useful item when accompanied by a map. Even generally knowing where you are and being oriented is a big part of being secure.

• Try to plan your arrival for the daytime, especially in unfamiliar cities and countries. Whenever possible, leave yourself several hours of daylight to locate your accommodations and get settled in.

Dealing with unwanted attention

Before we proceed, let's assume that not *all* attention automatically is unwanted nor is every unsolicited conversation a stranger strikes up a bad thing. You're smart enough to make your own judgment calls about where that line is. This section is only meant to address attention that *is* unwanted and to offer a few strategies for dealing with it.

It's a fact of life for women who travel alone: You attract attention you don't want. In many parts of the world, the people who live there don't consider it rude for a man to whistle at a woman, call out to her and/or comment to her at length about her attractiveness, often in very descriptive terms. If you're not prepared for a certain amount of this behavior in the world at large, you should travel with a companion.

There are three levels of unwanted attention: the passing comment, whistle or look; personal contact in the form of a stranger striking up a conversation; and physical contact — the pinch, pat or grope.

These are, to varying degrees, annoyances more than threats to your physical safety. The physical stuff is right on the borderline, of course, and should be treated accordingly, depending on the situation and the extent of the offense. Here are some tips for dealing with these different degrees of unwanted attention:

• The best way to react to a whistle, a passing comment, or lascivious stare or gesture is *not* to react. Ignore it. The vast majority of men who do these things are looking for a reaction — *any* reaction — and will leave it at that if they don't get one. Don't play.

- What about unwanted conversations? Experienced women travelers are used to being approached by men who want to strike up a conversation. Sometimes it's a pleasant diversion; often it's just a nuisance. Many of us were raised to "be polite" and have a hard time telling someone to buzz off — even when we really feel like it, and they really need to be told. But knowing how to terminate unwanted conversations is a useful skill (and good assertiveness training) for women who travel alone.

- For starters, remember this: You don't *have* to talk to someone if you don't want to. You don't have to answer their questions or tell them anything about yourself, where you're from, or where you're going. In short, you don't have to suffer fools gladly.

- Some people don't accept subtle cues or body language. Be assertive about breaking off conversations you don't want to have. This is your trip, your vacation. Having a book to read or a journal to write in can be a good deterrence to unwanted conversation. For the more persistent, be in control and firmly say any of the following:

   ✓ "Excuse me, but I want to be by myself."

   ✓ "Leave me alone."

   ✓ "Go away."

   ✓ "No!" (a universally recognized word)

And when I say be assertive, I mean *sound like you mean it.* If you're trying to sound friendly or polite to soften the blow, that's the only thing they'll hear.

- If all else fails, alter the existing dynamic. Walk away, raise your voice or do something that hopefully will embarrass or discourage the unwelcome party from pursuing their line of inquiry further.

- As for physical contact, choose your battles. The anonymous pinch on the bottom on a crowded city street may be extremely annoying but may not be worth creating a scene. For one thing, you may not even know who did it. Your starting point with more serious offenses should be an upraised hand, palm out and a loud, "No!" followed by any number of other possible words, depending on the situation.

- A common phenomenon is the subway masher, the jerk who uses the crush of a crowded subway car or platform as an excuse to fondle or grope a woman. These guys usually start with some sort of touching that's right on the border of what's obviously deliberate. If that doesn't elicit a reaction, they tend to be emboldened and push it to the next level. Don't tolerate this behavior. Call them on it. Raise your voice and embarrass them in front of other passengers, and get away from them as soon as you can.

PERSONAL SECURITY

I've traveled around the world for 20 years professionally, covering millions of miles — most of them by myself. I've traveled to 64 countries, many of them Third World countries. In all of that time and all of those miles, I've only been robbed once in my life. I'm a bit embarrassed to admit that it was in my own country. And it was because I wasn't paying attention.

Because I was home, my guard was down compared with my standard level of alertness and caution when traveling. So this is my No. 1 security tip above all else: Pay attention. Be aware of your surroundings. Here are some other practical tips for watching out for yourself when you're away from home:

- Don't walk around alone at night. Although this may seem obvious, we're sometimes lulled into a false sense of security by exotic locations and beautiful scenery.

- Trust your instincts. For example, don't get into an elevator alone with anyone who makes you uncomfortable. It's amazing how easily good manners sometimes get in the way of good common sense and gut reaction. If someone makes you apprehensive, even if you don't know why, pay attention to that feeling.

- Try to exude a calm, confident, no-nonsense air in public places. You may not always feel this way, but it actually works as a kind of force field. People will react to your cues, and sometimes just acting confident has a way of building confidence. It's very important for all travelers — and especially women travelers on their own — to have a good "game face."

- When you need to stop on a busy sidewalk to check your map or guidebook, stand with your back against a wall if possible. This lets you focus on what you're doing.

- If you're on the subway or train and feel nervous for some reason, sit next to another woman or seek out groups of women traveling together. Or sit next to a family or tourists who either are from your country or speak your language.

- Don't be too proud to ask for help if you need it. Most people in the world are people of good will and will help.

- Turn to other women for help in any situation where you feel the need.

Sad but true, most women have been alone and scared at one point or another, and they're willing to help — even if it's just letting you sit next to them on the train or the bus. Don't be shy about asking.

- Don't put yourself in potentially dangerous situations. Specifically, don't go off alone with a man you just met to a remote area or a room where you'll be alone.

- Be careful about your intake of alcohol. Don't let your guard down or your judgment slip when you're having a good time.

- Learn at least some rudimentary self-defense techniques before you travel alone. Take a class. Come to think of it, do this even if you don't travel.

- Don't travel with nice jewelry. It invites theft. It also invites resentment in poorer parts of the world, and you may lose something you don't want to lose.

- Don't make eye contact if you're in a situation that makes you feel uncomfortable.

- If you're driving alone, have a backup plan in case you get stranded, like using a cell phone.

- Don't wear shoes that restrict your mobility.

HOTEL SECURITY

- Ask to see the room. If it doesn't strike you as a securable room, don't take it.

- Bring a rubber doorstop to add security.

- Always use the deadbolt and other security features.

- Make sure the windows are secure.

- If you don't feel comfortable letting a male member of the service staff into your room, either don't open the door or leave it open and stand in the hall while he attends to whatever job he came to do.

- Don't leave your key on the table in the restaurant or the cafe, even if you're sitting right there. Many hotel keys have a plastic tag with the name of the hotel and the room number clearly visible on them. Don't advertise where you're staying and in what room.

- I recommend having your hotel key secured in such a way that it can't easily be lost or stolen, but is easily accessible so you can unlock and enter your room quickly.

ANOTHER WORLD: DIFFERENT CULTURES AND ATTITUDES

In many parts of the world, women traveling alone are so common that it elicits no comment or interest. But in many places in Asia, the Middle East and Africa, it's quite uncommon for a woman to travel without a male companion.

Wherever you go, whatever you do, know what to expect from the destination first. You may not agree with the local customs and attitudes, but you will have to live with them. Whether you agree with them or not is beside the point. You're still a foreign guest a long way from home, and some concessions to the local customs not only is good common sense, it's simply good manners.

If, for example, you are tempted to fly in the face of certain customs you don't agree with, you'd be better off not traveling to those countries to begin with. I'm not timid, just realistic. And I'm not suggesting that everyone should "go native," only that you be prepared to adapt your wardrobe to significantly different environments and customs.

Tips about clothing

For women, this almost always means covering up bare arms, bare legs and your head. So for more conservative countries (and certainly any Islamic country), I'd suggest bringing at least one of the following:

• A scarf to cover your head
• A long travel skirt (i.e., hemline below the knee)
• A long-sleeve shirt
• Long pants (or pants with zip-on-off legs)
• A selection of loose clothing that does a good job of concealment

Conveniences (or lack thereof), the facts of life and other delicate subjects (rated PG-13)

There are certain immutable facts of life and nature that shouldn't go unmentioned, though some readers might wish they would. Women, when you travel:

• Bring travel-size packs of tissues with you or bring an extra roll of toilet paper. Remove the cardboard from the roll and squish it to save space.
• Be prepared for your period wherever you go. Depending on where you travel, supplies may not be what you're used to or as readily available as you might hope/need. And travel can put you off your usual cycle. Be ready.

One solo woman traveler's perspective

 My friend, Mary, a thoroughly modern career woman, recently went to Istanbul, Turkey. Mary, an attractive, athletically built young woman with long blond hair, was traveling alone in a country where unattached, Western women are considered fair game and often hit on in some pretty overt ways.

Though she would have preferred to wear shorts and a sleeveless T-shirt in the hot Turkish sun, she strategically chose a wardrobe of loose-fitting cotton pants, long-sleeve shirts and below-the-knees travel skirts. And, for the most part, she also kept her long blond hair up or under a scarf.

"I'll admit I wasn't thrilled, feeling like I had to adjust my wardrobe and personal style as a precaution against being harassed or offending someone whose opinion I don't agree with," says Mary. "On the other hand, I'd flown thousands of miles to see these beautiful mosques where women have to cover up to get inside. In the end, it was just a practical decision. For years, I'd wanted to see Istanbul, and I didn't want to have to worry about constantly being badgered when I was walking down the street or having my access restricted. The wardrobe adjustment was a compromise that I made for the sake of my own safety and freedom of mobility."

CONCLUSION

My advice to women travelers who want to go it alone is this: Be smart, be careful and do your homework first, but go where you want to go. If you stay home because you're afraid of what *could* go wrong, then the jerks and the bad guys win by default.

Every activity that's worth doing carries some element of risk. We common-sense travelers do our best to reduce the risks — and certainly to eliminate all of the unnecessary ones — and then we go see the world. I'll see you out there.

CHAPTER 24

CULTURAL CONSIDERATIONS

*A myriad of miscommunications,
misunderstandings, missing manners
and missed opportunities
(and how to avoid such things)*

THE TWO MOST IMPORTANT THINGS

The two most important things you can pack for your trip are your respect for other people and your sense of humor. You'll need them both. Having respect for other people and other cultures doesn't mean compromising your own identity or cultural roots just to show the world how sensitive you are.

Be yourself, but . . .

Cultural sensitivity doesn't mean you have to walk on eggshells or be hypersensitive. It's fundamentally about common courtesy and a basic understanding — or *willingness* to understand — the people and places you encounter in the world.

All travelers are cultural ambassadors, whether they want the job or not. The golden rule is: Be as gracious a guest in someone else's country as you would want them to be in yours.

Let's take a look at some of the areas where cultures differ in ways that can lead to misunderstandings. Sometimes just knowing what to expect can make a world of difference in a world of *differences*.

Personal space

"Personal space" is one of those touchy-feely terms that's vaguely annoying but actually means something anyway. Basically, it's a fancy way of saying "the ideal distance you prefer to keep yourself from people you don't know."

For most North Americans in your average social situation, that's an arm's length or so. Other people in other countries sometimes have a more up-close-and-personal definition of personal space — usually because there's much less of it to go around where they live.

One thing's for certain, though: Travelers have to have a fairly elastic definition of the term, because the elbow room you'd prefer is not always the distance you have to deal with. Whether you ride the subway in Rome at rush hour, are the focus of a street vendor's persistent attention in Istanbul or find yourself clustered in a crowd at the Louvre to catch a glimpse of the Mona Lisa smile, at some point in your travels you're likely to find yourself in close quarters with other people.

Most of the time, the personal space incursions you encounter as a traveler aren't a cultural phenomenon so much as a byproduct of mass transportation and being drawn to popular destinations. That is to say, there's a big difference between someone who just happens to be in your space and someone who's too close for comfort. My advice is to be tolerant of the former but not the latter.

Language gaps: how (and how not) to bridge them

No one should be afraid to travel to a certain destination just because they're not fluent in the native tongue. When you cross borders, remember: Manners are an international language, and it doesn't take much of a vocabulary to be fluent in them.

A little bit of language can go a very long way. I recommend learning at least five words or basic phrases in the native tongue of any country you visit. It's amazing the difference such a small amount of language can make.

Most people are so gratified that you even care enough to make the effort to speak their language that they're very gracious and understanding about your lingual limitations. So, what five words or phrases should you learn? For starters, I recommend:

1. Hello

2. Excuse me

3. Please

4. Where is the bathroom?

5. Thank you

You'd be surprised how much bang you'll get for your linguistic buck. For example, you can mix and match your five words and phrases to come up with extremely useful new phrases such as, "Hello, excuse me: Where is the bathroom please? Thank you!"

Another great advantage of learning words and phrases in the native tongue is that many people in the world speak at least *some* English but are shy about trying it out. Let's face it, speaking to a stranger in a language that's not your own can be intimidating.

Many people around the world will be more helpful to you if you even make an effort to speak the words you know in their language. And they'll feel freer to try their English out on you. Sometimes that's a mixed blessing, but most of the time it's very helpful.

The one thing you always want to remember when you encounter the language barrier is not to butt your head against it. Though to some of you travelers this may seem obvious to the point of cliche, the first rule to remember is this: Volume does not equal comprehension.

If someone doesn't speak your language, speaking it more loudly will not do the trick. Sometimes speaking more *slowly* or clearly helps, but it's no guarantee. Should you ever find yourself in a foreign country bellowing at a fellow adult, take a moment, take a breath or take a step back and re-think your communication strategy.

Don't get me wrong, there definitely are what might be called volume-appropriate moments in certain situations. If someone just grabbed your bag and you're trying to get the attention of a nearby police officer, by all means, turn up the vocal volume — yell!

As for phrase books. I recommend keeping them as portable as possible and using the ones that are well-organized into specific phrases appropriate to specific locations, and that spell out words and phrases phonetically.

His and hers head-to-toe clothing tips

 **Head** — Women: Bring a scarf to cover your head when visiting places that require it (mosques, for example). Scarves don't take up any packing space, and they can prevent hassles. Men: Take your hat off before entering cathedrals, churches, etc., unless you're wearing a yarmulke in a synagogue (in which case, you obviously know what to do already).

Torso — Men and women: OK, it's hot and you want to wear a tank top. No problem. Just bring a light cotton long-sleeve shirt or a sweatshirt to wear inside the cathedral. Cathedrals can be very cool inside, even on hot days (lots of stone, shadows and high ceilings), so this is a practical comfort tip as well as a culturally appropriate one.

Legs — For both men and women, I suggest convertible pants with zip-off legs, which keep you cool but allow you to instantly convert between shorts and long pants.

Toes — Wearing casual sandals or flip-flops often is discouraged or forbidden at sacred sites. Bring along a pair of lightweight canvas sneakers to change into or just wear a comfortable pair of walking shoes that cover your feet. I consider a good, comfortable pair of walking shoes to be one of the most important parts of my wardrobe. A poorly fitting pair of shoes can keep you from taking advantage of all the sightseeing opportunities.

Oversized language dictionaries are not much help. Phrase books are extremely helpful, but keep in mind that your perfectly worded question read out of the phrase book often will elicit a perfectly worded response that you can't understand.

What to do? Focus on key words and be descriptive with your hands. English may be the international language, but panto-mime is the international I'm-sorry-I-don't-speak-the-language language. Try not to be shy. Many travel stores carry laminated cards with pictures of everything. They're useful for pointing to and showing someone what you need. Most are small enough to fit in your day bag.

Preventing culture shock

Culture shock is a broad term. Sometimes it's the butterflies in your stomach when you're trying to buy stamps and don't speak the language. Sometimes it's a form of homesickness or simply feeling overwhelmed by an environment that's completely different from the one you're used to. It happens from time to time.

What's the best way to prevent or minimize it? Learn before you leave:

• Read guidebooks about your destination.

• Try to at least browse a picture book or two about your destination.

• Learn a few key words and phrases in the native language.

• Study country and city maps for the places you're going to. Know the lay of the land, even if only generally. Bring portable, easy-to-handle maps. A small compass can be very helpful, too.

• Inform yourself about at least a few key cultural, historical and political facts about your destination.

Knowing what to expect or at least having some *idea* of what to expect when you arrive at your destination can do a lot to prevent culture shock and further your understanding of a place and the people in it. Sometimes it's surprising how little it really takes to feel at home when you're actually miles away from your own.

Observe these tips for food safety

"Cook it, wash it, peel it or forget it." Freshly cooked foods are less likely to acquire airborne contaminants. Raw foods such as salads and unpeeled fruits and vegetables are often likely culprits for trouble.

Nuts and other shelled foods are safe. Order portions well done or at least medium well and eat them only if served hot. Be especially careful of runny eggs. Condiments such as mayonnaise, ketchup and salad dressings are safest in sealed packages.

Cold-meat platters, cheese and buffet foods are often home to bacteria. Fish dishes are notorious for causing intestinal problems. Smaller fish tend to be safer. Shellfish such as clams, mussels and oysters are probably best avoided.

Avoid unpasteurized dairy products including cheese and yogurt. Check labels for evidence of pasteurization. Wash your hands before handling food. It's important that you use "safe" water to wash all food.

Go with the people flow — busy restaurants are usually the safest. The food is more likely to be fresh, clean and safe.

Sally Fernandez
AAA Travel Counselor
Columbia, S.C

CHAPTER 25

THE DELICATE ART
OF EFFECTIVE COMPLAINT

*If it ain't fixed
don't break it worse*

WHEN THINGS GO WRONG
Practice complaint triage

Triage is a medical term from the battlefield, meaning to sort out the wounded in order to determine treatment priority. It's a principle that can be applied to damage control in all sorts of circumstances. If something goes wrong — as some things inevitably do if you travel long enough — the first principle to remember is, don't make it worse. Suggestions:

- Whenever possible, try to resolve the issue on the spot by dealing with the person who's right in front of you. Can they solve the problem?

- If not, take it to the next level: Ask to see their supervisor or the manager on duty.

- f you've run your complaint all the way up the chain of command that's immediately available to you and still can't get the issue resolved, then you have to fight another day. This usually means pursuing your complaint higher up the ladder.

- To do this effectively, you must gather some key information.

Make a checklist of information to collect

No matter how carefully you plan, sometimes things go wrong. And whether a particular SNAFU was an act of God or a less divine form of interference, you'll still have to deal with it — usually on the spot, sometimes with additional follow-up efforts later on.

What types of problems are travelers most likely to encounter? Baggage delayed or lost. Flights missed, cancelled, delayed or overbooked. Hotel reservations mysteriously disappearing or accommodations that don't live up to what was promised. Unexpected or unexplained charges on a bill. Bad service at a restaurant. Take your pick.

But think before you complain. Will it actually help? There is no point in getting mad at the ticketing agent because bad weather delayed your flight. I assure you it's not their fault. However, if you made reservations for a two-bedroom suite with kitchen facilities and living room area for yourself and the family and you check in to find a room that resembles a phone booth with a cot in it… well, suffice it to say, you've got a case and it's time to go into complaint triage mode.

Whenever you encounter the dreaded "expectation gap" that requires action on your part, try to bear this in mind:

You can either blow off steam or you can gather the essential facts necessary to document what happened and have your grievances addressed. It's all very well to write an amazingly articulate letter of complaint to the corporate headquarters of the offending party, but it will accomplish nothing if you don't have your facts straight.

Remember the five Ws (who, what, why, where, when). You'll need all of them if you want to pursue a complaint effectively.

1. **Who** were you talking to? Or, if a particular individual is the issue, *who* was the problem? Get their name and, ideally, their manager's name, too. And remember to get the phone number.

2. **What** happened? Document the specific details of the problem or incident and what you want them to do about it. If there's something you specifically want, tell them. You may not get it, but you definitely won't get it if you don't ask.

3. **When** did it happen? You not only need the date, but also the time of day. If you're dealing with a personnel failure, it's very important to document what time of day the incident happened so that the party to whom you're complaining can narrow down who was on what shift.

4. **Where** did it happen? At the front desk? At the airline counter? In baggage claim? At the rental car company's downtown lot? Be specific — especially if you're dealing with any kind of chain or national/international company. Get the address, too.

5. **Why** are you so upset that you're writing or calling? Be specific. Effective complaints are a combination of presenting all the facts and also making it clear why a particular situation was so difficult or unfair or unacceptable.

Tip: Always travel with a pen and a small note pad. They're useful for more than just documenting the details of a problem so you can follow up on a complaint.

When there's a problem, who should you talk to?

Generally speaking, it's best to start with the person who's right in front of you: the desk clerk, the ticketing agent, the waiter, whoever. Don't automatically assume you have to go over their head. Give them a chance to do their job and sraighten out the problem Failing that, you should talk to their manager or supervisor (especially if the person you deal with is actually part of the problem). In the event you have to work your way up the chain of authority, keep track of the names and job titles of the people you talk to along the way and, whenever possible, get their business cards, too. Document as you go.

If you can't get the problem solved by talking to the personnel who are immediately available on site, you may have to live to fight another day. If you're dealing with any business that's part of a larger chain — such as hotels, restaurants or an airline — then you should write or call their customer service department, or even the president. Check out their website, get the number and the address. E-mailing or phoning can produce results, but you should be prepared to write a letter. Truth is, most companies realize that a customer who's upset enough to take the time to write a letter is a customer who's upset enough to stop patronizing their business. Nothing says "I'm upset. Really." quite like a good old-fashioned letter of complaint.

But whether you call, e-mail or use snail mail, be ready with the facts, the aforementioned Five W's. Most companies atually do want to keep the customer happy and ferret out the people or processes in their organization that screw things up, but it's not possible to do that if they don't have the information necessary to redress you grievance. Keep track of it and pass it on.

Don't kill the messenger

In ancient Greece, messengers who brought bad news were put to death, which was a high price to pay just for being the person who happened to have the information. Things have mellowed since then, but there's still a lesson to be learned.

Common-sense travel tip: Learn to distinguish between people who are only delivering bad news and the people or the *circumstances* that caused it. This way you don't take your annoyance out on someone who doesn't deserve it and who may be the only person who is in an immediate position to help you.

Be assertive but not rude

It's important to understand the difference between rudeness and assertiveness. You can be assertive without being rude, and I highly recommend this practice as an extremely effective traveler's strategy. Polite assertiveness is a skill. Rudeness, whether it's coming from the customer or service personnel, is a form of incompetence. Always start with good manners.

Good manners are practical. They are good common sense. And good manners combined with assertiveness will get you what you want — even in a bad situation — far more often than being rude.

Why is that?

What to do when you run into a service issue

1. If you encounter a problem either on the phone or in person, ask to speak to someone in authority.

2. If a hotel, car rental company, tour company or cruise line is unable to provide what you were promised, ask for a rate adjustment or a refund.

3. Be specific and reasonable with your request and say it with a smile.

4. Write everything down: the name of the person you spoke to, the time you spoke to him and what was said. You can take it one step further and have the person you spoke to sign it.

5. Pay for items with a credit card, that way if you had a complaint and were not able to resolve it, you can contest the charge with your credit card company when you get home.

Pamela Jordan Handley
AAA Travel Services Marketing Director
Independence, Ohio

Because the people you may be most inclined to yell at in the heat of the moment (the counter personnel on duty, for example) may be the only ones who can help you out of the jam their airline, hotel or rental car company put you in.

In short, whenever you encounter an expectation gap, don't start out mad. You always can go there if you need to, but give courtesy a shot first — it often works wonders. I'm not saying that being mad is the same thing as being rude. It isn't. But if you start out hopping mad when a problem arises, there's nowhere to go from there. Leave yourself some headroom.

CHAPTER 26

WHERE TO TURN

*Collected resources
and information*

This chapter includes useful contact information — addresses, phone numbers, websites — should an emergency arise when you're traveling internationally. An "I don't know what happened, but I'm in fairly serious trouble" kind of emergency. We don't mean to imply that you would intentionally commit a crime or flout international law, but you may accidentally break a rule or regulation in a distant country and find yourself in dire straits. This information explains who to turn to. Also included are health hotlines, full-service websites and other valuable contacts to help you plan your trip and prepare for the best.

TRAVEL INFORMATION

U.S. Department of State Contact Information
2201 C St. N.W., Washington, DC 20520
(202) 647-4000 • www.state.gov
Overseas Citizens Services 24-Hour Hotline: (202) 647-5225

Travel Warnings and Consular Information Sheets
travel.state.gov/travel_warnings.html

TRAVEL DOCUMENTATION

Passport Information

Bureau of Consular Affairs Passport Services
Room 6811, Washington, DC 20520
(900) 225-5674 with automated menu at 35 cents per minute
or operator assistance at $1.05 a minute
(888) 362-8668 ($4.95 flat fee)
travel/state/gov/passport_services.html

Visa Information

Public Inquiries/Visa Services
U.S. Department of State
Washington, D.C. 20522-0106
(202) 663-1225 • travel.state.gov/foreignentryreqs.html

Foreign Embassies in the United States

www.embassy.org/index.html

INTERNATIONAL TRAVEL HEALTH INFORMATION

Travelers' Health Hotline
(877) FYI-TRIP • www.cdc.gov/travel

Check out the latest government-issued health warnings by specific destination and find out about necessary vaccines.

World Health Organization
Avenue Appia 20, 1211 Geneva 27, Switzerland
(+00 41 22) 791 21 11 • E-mail: info@who.int _ www.who.int/home-page

The WHO's website provides a great deal of information, with an emphasis on alerting the world traveler to potential health risks and preventing disease outbreaks.

TRANSPORTING GOODS, CUSTOMS
United States Customs Service
1300 Pennsylvania Ave. N.W.
Washington, D.C. 20229
(202) 927-6724 • www.customs.ustreas.gov/

Bureau of Alcohol, Tobacco and Firearms
Office of Liaison and Public Information
650 Massachusetts Ave. N.W., Room 8290
Washington, D.C. 20226
www.atf.treas.gov

IMMIGRATION
U.S. Immigration and Naturalization Service (INS)
United States Department of Justice
425 I St. N.W., Washington, DC 20536-0003
(800) 375-5283 or (202) 307-1501 • www.usdoj.gov/ins/

GENERAL TRAVEL INFORMATION
Whether you are just beginning to explore your options or are ready to book the reservations, the following full-service websites provide a combination of information and services for travelers in every stage of planning.

America the Beautiful
National Park Foundation
www.nationalparks.org/index.html

This nonprofit partner of the National Parks Service has a site devoted to encouraging patronage through information and photos. Order a National Parks Pass online, and you and a carload of people can gain access to any national park for a year.

National Scenic Byways Program
www.byways.org

Find the 72 designated National Scenic Byways of America, recognized by the Secretary of Transportation as being notable for their "archaeological, cultural, historic, natural, recreational and scenic qualities."

Tourstates.com
www.tourstates.com

Traveling in the United States? Pick a state, and the official website of the National Council for State Tourism Directors can link you directly to the tourism office for your destination.

Roadsideamerica.com
www.roadsideamerica.com/index.html

This is an amusing, offbeat guide to the quirkiest of tourist attractions listed by name or by state. If you're wondering where the National Plastics Museum is located, this is the site for you. (P.S. It's in Leominster, Mass.)

HIGHWAY AND WEATHER CONDITIONS

U.S. Department of Transportation
Federal Highway Administration
Nassif Building
400 Seventh St. S.W., Washington, D.C. 20590
7:45 a.m. to 4:15 p.m. • www.fhwa.dot.gov

Information about construction and weather-related car and transit conditions nationwide, with links to regional sites.

AIR TRAVEL

Federal Aviation Administration
www.faa.gov

The FAA's site includes a great deal of useful information about safety, baggage restrictions and airport security.

Air Traffic Control System Command Center
www.fly.faa.gov/flyFAA/index.html

This site provides airport flight delay information in real time, updated every five minutes.

RAILROAD AND RAILPASS INFORMATION

Amtrak
(800) USA-RAIL • www.amtrak.com/

Via Rail Canada
3 Place Ville-Marie, Suite 500
Montreal, Quebec H3B 2C9, Canada
(888) VIA-RAIL • www.viarail.ca

Eurail
www.eurail.com

Rail Europe
www.raileurope.com/us/index.htm

This site has information about the many European rail systems and passes, including Eurail, BritRail and the France Railpass. You also can book reservations and purchase your passes online.

HELPFUL TRAVEL CONVERSION SITES

YourDictionary.com
www.yourdictionary.com/index.shtml

This site has 260 different language dictionaries online and counting.

CHAPTER 27

THE RETURN TRIP

Re-entry duties and declarations,
what to bring home and how to get it there,
what not to bring home,
and what's the deal
with duty-free shopping anyway?

OF DUTIES AND DECLARATIONS

What you have to pay for, what you don't and how to know the difference

Duty. Duty-free items. Customs declaration forms. Personal exemptions. It can all get a bit confusing sometimes — especially if it's new to you. But even among the well-traveled, many people would have a hard time if they were pressed to explain, for example, what "duty-free" means and why duty-free shops are like little boutiques for guilty pleasures and legal vice.

Will you have to pay duty on the stuff you're bringing home? And if so, how much? Is "duty-free" really duty-free? Are there ways you can protect yourself from paying too much duty (and other taxes) on goods you're bringing back? Should you have shipped it home instead? If so, how? And what's OK to bring back to the United States, and what isn't?

Let's start with the basics.

What is duty?

Duty is just a name for the tax that's collected on imported goods, that is, certain items that you bring into a country you're visiting or take with you when you return home from overseas. Duty rates vary, depending on the item, where it was made and how expensive it is. Dutiable items must be declared at customs.

Checklist of things you must declare

- Anything you purchased and are carrying with you when you return to the United States.
- Gifts you received while you were out of the country (including wedding presents and birthday presents).
- Gifts you're bringing home for someone else.
- Items you inherited.
- Any items purchased in a duty-free shop, on the plane or on the ship.
- Items you're bringing home for somebody else.
- Any repairs or alterations to any items taken abroad and then brought back (even if these repairs or alterations were done for free).
- Items you're bringing home to sell or use for your business.

What is the customs declaration form, and what are you supposed to do with it?

The customs declaration is a form on which you list all of the dutiable items (all the things you're bringing home that you didn't have with you when you left) and the price you paid for them so that customs can assess how much duty, if any, you owe.

If you're traveling by plane or by ship, a customs declaration form almost always is handed out on the return trip. If you're traveling by car, you should consider picking up a customs declaration form at the post office before your trip if you know you'll have stuff to declare on the way home.

Filling out the customs declaration form will be much easier if you save your receipts and pack the items you must declare separately. (See *What to bring home (and how to get it there),* below, for further details.)

If you don't have the receipts, don't fudge on the price. Customs officials usually are as gifted at appraisals as an auctioneer at Sotheby's. If you try to pull a fast one on customs, you could forfeit your undeclared or undervalued item(s) and also be subject to a fine.

If you're not sure whether or not to declare something, do it anyway. Remember: Just because you declare an item, it doesn't automatically mean that duty will be assessed on it.

How do you declare them?

Using the customs declaration form, write down the items you're declaring and the price you paid for them, including the tax. Customs doesn't want to do the math for you, so you have to write the value of dutiable items down in U.S. currency equivalents.

If you're declaring an item you received as a gift but don't know the price of it, you should make your best guess or have the gift appraised in the country you received it in before you head home.

What's a duty-free exemption?

A duty-free exemption (also known as a personal exemption) refers to the total value of goods you're allowed to bring back into the country without having to pay duty on them. For returning U.S. residents, the personal exemption almost always is $400, though there are restrictions that apply to alcohol and tobacco products. You can use your $400 exemption once every 30 days.

Duty-free exemption rates vary depending on how long you've been out of the country and what country you're returning from. And it can be worth it to know the exceptions to the rule.

For example, there are a lot of countries in Central America and the Caribbean basin where you get a higher personal exemption rate. For specific details, I recommend contacting U.S. Customs or — faster still — checking out their website, which has a chart of different countries and corresponding duty-free exemption amounts for travelers returning from those countries. (Contact information for U.S. Customs is provided in Chapter 26.)

A problem you'll want to avoid (and how to avoid it)

How does customs know that your brand new, foreign-made, state-of-the-art $3,000 laptop or that nice new watch your spouse gave you for your birthday isn't something you picked up on your trip overseas?

They don't.

And they can make you pay duty on items you already own if you can't prove they're yours, right on the spot. Is this fair? Sort of. People do try to scam customs all the time by pretending pricey items they bought overseas actually are personal items they've had with them all along.

On the other hand, it isn't fair for you to pay duty on stuff that already is yours. Customs doesn't operate on the "innocent until proven guilty" principle. When it comes to declaring goods at customs, the burden of proof is on the traveler, period, so you have to be prepared.

Here's what you can do

You can bring documentation along with you that proves a given item was yours before you left on your trip. Acceptable forms of proof include sales receipts, insurance policies and jeweler's appraisals.

Or you can register these items with customs before you even leave home.

MONEY-SAVING TIP NO. 1

Register personal items with U.S. Customs before you leave

The following items are among the consumer goods you can register:

• Watches and jewelry

• Laptops

• Cameras

• CD players

Any item you register must have what customs calls "unique, permanent markings" or serial numbers. Items can be registered at any customs office. Once there, request a certificate of registration, Customs Form 4457.

Customs has to see the items being registered in order for them to certify your certificate of registration. Once items are registered and your form is certified, those items will be duty-exempt as long as you bring your certified certificate of registration with you when going through customs.

This whole process can be taken care of at the customs station in the international airport you're leaving from. Certified certificates of registration are reusable for future trips, so you don't have to register your laptop every time you go overseas.

The duty-free shop

Duty-free shops can be confusing places, starting with their own name. There's a common misconception that you don't ever have to pay duty on goods purchased in a duty-free shop. Logical, right?

But not necessarily true.

Still a bit confused? Who wouldn't be? Duty-free shops definitely can induce a sort of border dyslexia. So here's the rule about paying duty on duty-free stuff, straight from the source (the United States Customs Service):

Articles sold in a duty-free shop are free of duty and taxes only for the country in which that shop is located. So if your purchases exceed your personal exemption, items you bought in a duty-free shop, whether in the United States or abroad, almost certainly will be subject to duty.

What all of that means is this: If you bought a $500 watch at the duty-free shop in the Amsterdam airport, you'd still have to pay duty on some of it when you returned to the United States, that is, duty would be owed on the $100 of the watch's price that's over your $400 personal exemption.

Here's another example of how the rule works: If you bought a bottle of expensive perfume at the duty-free shop in Champlain, N.Y., before crossing into Québec, Canada, and then you returned home to the United States with that same bottle of expensive perfume, it could be subject to duty.

So, all of this begs the question: *Is the duty-free shop a good deal?* Not necessarily. Duty-free means that you're not paying the import tax normally imposed on those goods by the country you're purchasing them in. It doesn't automatically mean it's a bargain — especially if you have to pay duty later.

There definitely are good deals to be found here and there in the duty-free shops of the world. But you still have to bargain hunt just as you would in any other retail environment (including the factory outlet stores you find on the border).

The truth is, duty-free shops flourish whether they offer bargains or not, because international travelers get bored during layovers and can't resist spending what's left of their foreign currency.

MONEY SAVING TIP NO. 2

Getting your money's worth at the duty-free shop

The best way to get a good deal at the duty-free shop is to purchase only those items you know are going for a good price — and only if those items won't put you over your $400 personal exemption.

What not to bring home

This is by no means a complete list. There are many items (such as firearms or live animals) that can be brought into the United States, but require special permits to do so. For inquiries about such things, I recommend directing your questions directly to U.S. Customs or getting more detailed information from their website.

However, these are some common items that you'll want to avoid bringing back into the country:

1. Perishable fruits and vegetables

2. Meat (including fresh, dried, canned and meat products)

3. Illegal drugs

4. Drug paraphernalia

5. Any products made from any endangered species; any part of any endangered species

6. Products made from or with dog or cat hair

7. Plants (even though there are exceptions to this rule, but they require a permit)

8. Merchandise from embargoed countries, including Afghanistan, Cuba (including Cuban cigars — even if you bought them legally in Canada), Iran, Iraq, Libya, Serbia and Sudan

9. Cultural artifacts and cultural property

10. Absinthe (a yucky green liquid that rots your brain, favored by 19th century poets)

ALCOHOL, TOBACCO, FIREARMS AND OTHER HEALTH HAZARDS

Some items may not be illegal, but the rules that govern their transport across borders are much stricter. Not surprisingly, these items are the domain of the Bureau of Alcohol, Tobacco and Firearms (contact information provided at the end of the chapter).

There are a few basic things you should know about these items. For example, you can't allot your entire $400 personal duty-free exemption for alcohol (or tobacco).

Alcohol

Your personal exemption can include one liter (33.8 fluid ounces) of alcoholic beverages if you are 21 years old, it's for personal use or being given as a gift, and it doesn't violate the laws of the state you're crossing into.

Tobacco

If, like most people, your personal exemption is $400, this entitles you to purchase up to 200 cigarettes or 100 cigars duty-free.

Firearms

Needless to say, this is a very complicated area of international law. Many countries will not let you bring in a gun, even if you're just passing through. Hunting rifles are allowed in some places, but are strictly regulated. And, of course, firearms and ammunition being brought back into the United States also are strictly regulated.

Never assume anything is just OK. For details about the specific rules and regulations, contact customs and the ATF (information is at the end of the chapter).

WHAT TO BRING HOME (AND HOW TO GET IT THERE)

What can you bring home with you? Pretty much anything, as long as it's legal, you're prepared to pay duty on it, and you can get it there. Here are some good ways to get your purchases home, and some tips for saving yourself a lot of money and hassle in the process.

MONEY SAVING TIP NO. 3

Keep track of your receipts and merchandise

• Save all of your receipts in an envelope or resealable plastic bag.

Things to know about prescription medication when traveling abroad

1. Always declare your prescription medicine.
2. Prescription drugs always should be carried in their original containers.
3. Bring the amount you'll need for the duration of your trip, but don't bring a significant amount more.
4. Either carry a copy of your prescription with you or a written statement from your doctor, verifying that your medication is being taken under a doctor's supervision and is necessary for your health and well-being.
5. Ask your drugstore, doctor or pharmacist if they can print a copy of your prescription translated into the language of the countries you'll be traveling to. Many of them can. Call around and find one who does.

- When you get a receipt, write the U.S. equivalent of the value on the receipt immediately. It's a lot easier to figure out the exchange rate a receipt at a time as you make your purchases than it is to try and calculate them all at once when you arrive at customs and have to fill out the customs declaration form.
- Keep your receipts in your tote bag with your declarable items.
- Just hand the whole package off to customs: Here's what I bought. Here's how much I paid for it.

Rules about sending stuff home

Sometimes shipping stuff home is a necessity, but it can be expensive. Aside from the shipping costs, many international express carriers, for example, charge fees to clear your packages through customs.

- You can't prepay duty on items you ship home. They are subject to duty when they arrive, and you can't include them in your personal exemption.
- You still have to pay duty on items purchased overseas even if you ship them home.
- You're allowed to send up to $100 a day in gifts to individuals. Packages should be labeled "unsolicited gift," and you should write

what the gift is and how much it's worth on the package. You also can send a consolidated gift package as long as each gift is individually wrapped and labeled. If any one gift is more than $100, however, duty will be assessed on the contents of the entire package. The outside of the package should be labeled "consolidated gift package," and each individual recipient's name, their gift and its value also should be written on the package. These gifts do not have to be declared at customs when you return home.

- What about sending your own personal belongings home? To avoid paying duty, write "American goods returned" on the package. The items must be of U.S. origin.

Money-saving tip No. 4: Get GST and VAT refunds

GST stands for goods and service tax. VAT means value-added tax. These are sales taxes found around the world that are meant for residents, not visitors from other countries. Did you know that these taxes often are refundable at the border? It's true, and it can save you a bundle of money on your purchases.

There are exceptions to the rule that you should know about first. The GST/HST is not refundable on items such as alcohol, food and beverages, tobacco, transportation, entertainment, automobile fuel and certain services, such as dry cleaning, for example.

But you can get money back on most manufactured goods purchased. To get your refund, save your receipts and turn them in at participating land border duty-free shops (in most countries). You'll have to fill out a rebate form that accompanies your receipts, and generally you're refunded on the spot.

There usually is a minimum purchase amount required per each receipt for you to be eligible for a GST/HST refund. This amount can range from $50 to several hundred dollars. In Canada, for example, each receipt must be for $50 or more (before tax), and you also must have a total minimum of $200 in purchases to get a rebate.

Rebate forms generally are available at duty-free shops, tourist information centers, customs offices, hotels and from many merchants.

CHAPTER 28

COMMITTING YOUR TRIP TO MEMORY

*How to remember
what you wouldn't want
to forget*

HOLD THAT THOUGHT

Seeing the world usually makes a strong impression. In the days immediately following your return home, travel memories are so vivid you think you'll never forget them. But unless you have some sort of system for documenting your memories, a lot of them do get lost as time passes.

The exact date you were in "what-was-that-great-place?"; the name of the person you had that interesting conversation with on the train; the street address of that amazing Indian restaurant you found in London — the details are the first to go.

Sometimes the essence of a trip is captured in a photo, sometimes by the written word and sometimes by something as small as a ticket stub. Whatever details stand out as the ones that matter to you, preserve them.

BEFORE YOU GO ON YOUR TRIP

• When you're planning a trip, remember to set aside some of your travel budget for film, film development, scrapbooks and supplies such as pens, paper, scissors, glue.

• If possible, buy scrapbooks and supplies before you leave home and have everything ready to put together in a scrapbook as soon as you return. It's a nice way to extend the trip and to relive it.

TIPS FOR DOCUMENTING YOUR TRAVELS

Photographic memories

Whether you're an expert photographer with top-of-the-line equipment or a college student on a tight budget using a disposable camera, you'll thank yourself later if you take the time to take pictures of your trip.

Here's some tips to remember:

• Buy your film before you leave home.

• Get your film developed as soon as you get home.

• Don't just photograph famous monuments and buildings when you travel. Take pictures of the people you meet, too. You always can buy a postcard of the Eiffel Tower or the Coliseum. When you're taking pictures, try to capture the truly unique elements of your trip that will never repeat themselves. Hundreds of pictures of buildings can feel cold and impersonal no matter how dramatic they seemed at the time.

• When you're photographing the locals, it's often a good idea to ask permission to take their picture beforehand. Many people aren't

Keep a travel journal

Travel journals are a wonderful way to keep memories of your journey, but they can be heavy to pack and can seem like a homework assignment at the end of a long day of sight-seeing. My mother continually reminded me to keep a travel journal for my personal reference of all the exciting places I was going and all my adventures, but I was always too busy having fun to stop and "journal."

Fast forward 15 years. Over the years, I kept in touch with my family by sending postcards from around the world. Guess what? They kept every postcard I sent and gave them back to me in boxes! I'm thrilled! I now have all those fantastic memories as keepsakes.

Here's what I suggest: Purchase inexpensive postcards of your favorite sights, historical and cultural — and most hotels have their own postcards — and jot down a quick note on the back. Write about a special memory of the day, a favorite restaurant and its location, a terrific tour guide and their contact information for future reference. Anything that strikes your fancy that day. Then purchase the most interesting stamp you can find and mail the postcard.

To yourself!

Not only do I preserve great memories in this way, but it's faster and more enjoyable than a travel journal. I can pop a few postcards in my day bag and write them while I'm having lunch. Or riding a train through the countryside.

And best yet, I receive mail when I get home! It's fun to see how long it takes to receive mail from different parts of the world.

Here's what I do with these pieces of mail. I punch a hole in an upper corner and tie a ribbon around all the cards from my trip and place them on my coffee table. Not only is it a good conversation piece, but it keeps all the cards together. After a time, I place the neatly organized postcards into a shoe box — that I've decorated with maps — and catalog by the trip. It's an easy reference for me, but also when a friend asks, "What was the name of that great restaurant you raved about in Florence?" I have the answer ready.

comfortable having their picture taken or being made to feel like a tourist attraction. And as wonderful as it is to have pictures of your trip, there definitely are times when it's best not to take a picture. Sometimes just the act of taking a picture distances you from the immediacy of the moment or the person you're interacting with — as if to say, "I'm not really part of this; I'm just stopping in to take a photo." I'm not trying to be a killjoy. I'm just suggesting that you use your own best judgment about this.

- Don't go through customs with film in your camera. While it's very rare for customs officials to expose your rolls of film, they may open your camera. What's their policy about this? I'll quote U.S. Customs: "Customs will not examine film you bought abroad and are bringing back unless the customs officer has reason to believe it contains prohibited material."

- "Will the airport X-ray machine ruin my film?" This is a question that never seems to be settled. That's because there isn't any one answer. In North America and Europe, it's safe to leave your film in your *carry-on* bag when your bag is being X-rayed. (If you're traveling through Third World airports, it's usually a good idea to hand over your film to security personnel and have them look it over rather than sending it through the X-ray machine.) However, you shouldn't leave undeveloped film in your *checked* bags any more because of the high-intensity X-ray machines being used to screen bags for nasty things like explosives. These machines are good news for security, but bad news for your film. Plan accordingly.

- One final suggestion: Don't spend so much time trying to document the perfect moment that you actually miss it while it's happening.

Putting it into words

- Every picture tells a story, but nothing tells the whole story like the written word. Bring a couple of pens and pencils and at least one small notebook with you when you travel to keep a trip journal.

- Don't worry about trying to make your journal writing perfect. Try to capture the important details of your trip, even if you're only making rough notes. You always can flesh out your journal when you get home.

- Write down the names of the places where you stay and the people you meet — all of the things that you're most likely to forget first.

- If you're sending e-mails to friends along the way, keep copies for yourself. E-mails to others can make a very good addition to a trip journal or your scrapbook.

- Bring a mini-cassette recorder with you for those times when you can't write. Mini-cassette tapes always can be used to fill out the details in a travel journal later on.

Scrapbook tips

- My best advice for making a good scrapbook of your trip is to be creative about the contents. You don't have to limit yourself to photos. You can put anything in there that captures the essence of your trip: colorful paper money from foreign countries, postcards, ticket stubs, a page from your journal, a cocktail napkin, a coaster from that great

I wish I had ...

1. Checked the camera for film. Many wonderful pictures are only a memory when the camera isn't loaded!
2. Packed an inflatable pillow in my carry-on bag to make naps more comfortable.
3. Packed an extra folding tote bag for purchases and gifts.
4. Bought a much-wanted souvenir and shipped it home, so it doesn't take up space in a suitcase.
5. Packed ear plugs so I can get to sleep.
6. Packed toilet paper. No need to explain.
7. Packed a towel for bathing, beaching or picnicking.
8. Worn comfortable walking shoes and taken Band-Aids and Second Skin for little emergencies.
9. Brought No-Jet-Lag homeopathic tablets and Airborne herbal health formula to fight jet lag and airborne illnesses.
10. Brought bubble pack to protect breakable souvenirs and gifts for the journey home.
11. Packed clothes using compression bags to save space. They can also be used to bring back dirty clothes.
12. Packed patience, especially with the long lines at airport security. Safety is of the utmost importance and delays are inevitable. Learn to relax, breathe and get to know the people around you.

Colleen Coe, Manager
AAA Oregon/Idaho Travel Stores
Portland, Ore.

pub in Edinburgh, colorful matchbook covers (tear out the bulky matches first), a pressed flower, the slip of paper your new friends wrote their e-mail addresses on or anything else that brings the trip back for you.

- On the back of photos, write the date, place and any other specifics you wouldn't want to forget. Or, better yet, if you're mounting photos in your scrapbook so that they're not removable, write your own separate photo captions and include them in the scrapbook. You also can use pages (or copies of pages) from your travel journal to accompany your trip photos.

- As you travel, store your scrapbook memorabilia in one or more resealable plastic bags to keep it from getting scattered or damaged.

- Use Ziploc freezer bags so you can write the name of each city (or country) on each bag to keep things organized.

- Before you even leave home, set up a good workspace for putting your scrapbook together. Have all the tools you need ready and waiting for you when you get home: pen, paper, scissors, glue, two-sided tape and scrapbooks.

Nice memories — and how soon can we go again?

Good documentation is not just a way to preserve memories, it also serves as a reminder of why you went in the first place. And it's a great incentive to take more trips and to make more good memories in the future.

Living life to the fullest, gaining a greater understanding of the world, remembering to have fun, spending time with family, making good memories — these are the things that travelers' dreams are made of. And they deserve to be preserved and relived. Not only in memory, but again in the very near future.

AFTERWORD

Arc de Triomphe — discoveries and rediscoveries of travel

One day, to my astonishment, I actually won a contest. The prize was a humdinger: two round-trip tickets to anywhere in the world. Needless to say, I was thrilled. Visions of exotic destinations kaleidoscoped through my mind — Kenya, Fiji, Machu Picchu, New Zealand, Beijing. Suffice it to say, I had a long list. *Anywhere in the world* opened up all sorts of possibilities.

Feeling incredibly lucky, I decided to share my good fortune (that is, the other ticket) with one of my closest friends. To add to the treat, I told her she could pick the destination. I've spent my life traveling around the world both personally and professionally, and it just seemed like the thing to do to let my friend choose the destination. She chose…Paris.

I'm a little embarrassed to admit that I felt disappointed, though I kept it to myself, of course. Don't get me wrong: I love Paris. Always have, always will. But in the course of my travels, I'd been there many times already. I guess you could say that I'd developed just a little bit of a "been there, done that" attitude. The Eiffel Tower? Been there. Notre Dame? Done that.

Silly me. As if the sum total of a country's monuments somehow could be the whole picture. Even seasoned travelers lose perspective sometimes. This is the story of how I regained mine.

On the flight over, I found myself thinking back to my first incredible trip to Paris and the way I felt the day I saw that glorious city for the first time. It had been a particularly dramatic introduction.

I was a student at the time, taking a bike tour across Europe with 27 fellow students. Paris was the last stop on our eight-week tour, which had begun in Vienna. I remember that we actually stopped traffic on the Champs-Elysees as we took a triumphant victory lap around the Arc de Triomphe, streamers flying from our handlebars. It was a wonderful, perfect moment — a glorious day and the thrill of a lifetime.

Now, all these years later, my friend and I had cashed in my prize, and I was back in Paris showing her the sights. We were riding a crowded Metro train to the Arc de Triomphe, and privately I was feeling that it would be a bit anticlimactic compared to my memory of that day long ago.

As we climbed the stairs from the metro stop, we encountered a large crowd of people gathered around the monument — larger than usual, that is to say. As we strolled closer to the crowd, a policeman suddenly blew his whistle and started to push people back. The first thought that came to my mind was, "Is this a demonstration or protest?"

But no, it looked like some sort of ceremony. Standing next to us were two middle-age men, both accompanied by two younger men who seemed to be their sons. As it turned out, they were Americans and, hearing us speak English, they struck up a conversation and explained to us what was happening: The eternal flame was being ceremonially "re-lit" in remembrance of soldiers lost or fallen in the war. Unknowingly, we'd arrived right in the middle of the ceremony.

A mournful-sounding trumpet played, and a drum beat out a slow, methodic pulse while, to our left, about 20 French veterans approached in full dress uniform — *original* uniforms — some a little tight around the middle, but all perfectly pressed and adorned with medals.

Some of the veterans were walking hand in hand with young children (presumably grandchildren), all dressed in their Sunday best. The veteran at the front of the procession carried a large wreath, which he placed at the base of the flame. A few quiet words were spoken and then it was over, just like that. The entire ceremony lasted maybe 10 minutes. But while it was going on, everyone was completely silent, spellbound by this extraordinary scene of quiet dignity.

Afterward, as the crowd drifted away, we thanked our new acquaintances who had explained what was happening, and we learned why they were there. They also were veterans as it happened, veterans of the Vietnam War. And, they told us, they had planned their entire trip to Europe around this ceremony and had brought their sons with them to instill in them a respect for veterans and fallen soldiers. Our accidental experience was, for them, the crowning moment of their trip.

We parted company and never saw them again. But I'll never forget that day and how it put my life and my travels into perspective. The dignity of those veterans from two very different wars. The gravity of their experiences pulling us into the place and the moment so unexpectedly, but so completely. To me it was a reminder that places — even the ones we think we "know"— renew themselves every day because of the people in them and the things that happen there. So, while I was disappointed at the onset, as my friend chose Paris, you can guess who had the best time.

These are the moments that the traveler instinctively seeks, often without even knowing they're doing it. You won't find such moments in a guidebook, and you can't plan them ahead of time. You just have to have faith that they're out there waiting for you: those perfect moments when people and places converge seamlessly and something extraordinary happens.

Whatever you call it — serendipity, chance or fate — when it happens to you, smile to yourself and know that it's your lucky day.

INDEX